TEN
DATES
For MATES

TEN DATES
For MATES

Dave & Claudia Arp

THOMAS NELSON PUBLISHERS
Nashville · Camden · New York

To our three special sons
Jarrett, Joel and Jonathan
Thanks for your patience
as we worked on this book.
May you and your future wives someday
benefit from these pages.

Third printing

Published in Nashville, Tennessee, by Thomas Nelson, Inc. and distributed in Canada by Lawson Falle, Ltd., Cambridge, Ontario.

Printed in the United States of America.

Scripture quotations are from the *New American Standard Bible,* © The Lockman Foundation 1960, 1962, 1963, 1968, 1971, 1972, 1973, 1975, 1977, and are used by permission.

Book design by Nancy Bozeman

Library of Congress Cataloging in Publication Data

Arp, Dave.
   Ten dates for mates.

   Includes bibliographical references.
   1. Marriage. 2. Communication in marriage.
3. Dating (Social customs) 4. Marriage—Religious
aspects—Christianity. I. Arp, Claudia. II. Title.
HQ734.A69   1983   646.7'8   83-3954
ISBN 0-8407-5845-6

CONTENTS

ACKNOWLEDGMENTS

We want to express our appreciation to two couples whose continual encouragement has resulted in this book.

We thank Clark and Ann Peddicord for assisting in the birth of MARRIAGE ALIVE and their encouragement and help to keep it growing and developing all along the way.

We also thank Jody and Linda Dillow for their encouragement and excellent critique in writing TEN DATES FOR MATES and especially to Linda for her creative suggestions and tireless efforts in editing TEN DATES.

To these four very dear friends we say, "Thank you!" You are a vital part of this book.

FOREWORD

I'm excited about this book by Dave and Claudia Arp. My wife and I first met this couple in Vienna, Austria. We were in Europe for ministry, and had the opportunity to stay in their home. Casual encounters, of course, are not a valid basis for evaluation—but in our brief time with the Arps, Elaine and I sensed we had just met a couple with an above-average marriage. Later, our observations were verified by those who *had* known them well over a period of years.

When you read this book you'll understand why their marriage is above average. They have worked at their relationship. And because they have, they have certainly earned the right to share their ideas with others.

Yes, I'm excited about this book because it reflects an authentic couple who have something to share out of their own experience. But I'm also excited because the material is thoroughly biblical and intensely practical. The title *Ten Dates for Mates* actually tells the "structural" story. Each marital partner does a reading and writing assignment ahead of time! Then, they "go out together" and share their responses.

This book will help every couple grow in their marital relationship. My wife and I recommend it highly.

Gene A. Getz
Center for Church Renewal
Pastor, Fellowship Bible Church-North
Plano, Texas

A SPECIAL NOTE TO HUSBANDS
FROM DAVE

Your idea?

Are you looking for a special gift for your wife—perhaps for a birthday, an anniversary, Christmas, or a gift for no special reason at all? What can you give her that would be really special and unique? May I suggest a gift that may be hard to give but that will be much appreciated . . . a gift of time and of yourself!

Give your mate *ten dates*!

This can be a unique opportunity to strengthen and deepen your relationship and commitment to each other. This gift can have lasting effects long past the ten dates.

You might be thinking, "You mean actually have ten dates with my wife? What would we talk about?" Each date is already planned for you. You can follow our suggestions in detail or use them as a track to run on. We have tried to make them interesting, varied, and easy to prepare for.

Her idea?

Perhaps you've just come home from a busy day at work and your wife has presented you with this book and casually (?) asked, "Honey, how would you like to go through this book and have ten dates with me?" What's your response? Check one or more of the following:

_____ 1. I need help.

_____ 2. My wife thinks I need help!

_____ 3. My wife needs help.

_____ 4. My wife wants to spend time with me.

_____ 5. My wife wants me to commit myself to spend time with her.

_____ 6. It might be fun.

_____ 7. It can't hurt.

_____ 8. I have my doubts but I'll give it a try.

_____ 9. I am willing to invest ten dates in strengthening my relationship with my wife.

Remember, the difference between a rut and a grave is only a few feet!

A SPECIAL NOTE TO WIVES
FROM CLAUDIA

His idea?

If your husband found this book and handed it to you, suggesting that you spend ten special dates together, be exceedingly glad! With all of today's pressures few husbands will have the time to search out books or will take the initiative in making more time commitments.

If your husband came up with the idea first, don't take it as a subtle hint that he is unhappy with you. Instead, be excited that he wants to spend time with you and to commit himself to you in a new way. I hope your response will be, "Great! When is our first date?"

Your idea?

More likely, you are the one who has discovered this book and would love to experience ten dates with your mate. But perhaps you are afraid of rejection—that he won't have the time and will say no if you make the suggestion. What's a wife to do? If you want to live in Discouragement City, you could:

1. Not use the book and join the Poor Me Club.
2. Give it to your husband and say, "I know you aren't interested, but . . ."
3. Try to work through it alone and get totally discouraged.

Or perhaps you could be creative:

1. Present your husband with a coupon book of ten dates. Offer to make the physical arrangements (such as getting sitters). You will find a plan for each of the ten dates with helpful and practical suggestions.
2. Tell him how much you desire to spend time with him, that this book is not a subtle hint that you're dissatisfied with your relationship, but that it is an opportunity to continue to grow in intimacy together.
3. Pray that he'll say yes!

Remember, someone needs to take the first step. The greatest threat to marriage today is boredom and monotony. Be willing to be the initiator in adding spice to your married life!

AN IMPORTANT NOTE TO BOTH

What is Ten Dates for Mates?

Ten Dates for Mates is a unique opportunity for those couples who want to fine-tune their marriage, improve communication skills, and make a good marriage better. Ten special events have been planned for husband and wife, each building upon the previous one. Included are suggestions on where to go and what to do, so each date can be meaningful and helpful.

Who is it for?

Ten Dates for Mates is for:
—those with good communication who want to deepen it.
—those with poor communication who want to improve it.
Ten Dates for Mates is for couples who have good marriages and are committed to making them better still. A thriving marriage is characterized by growth and commitment. Perhaps your growth rate has slowed and you want the opportunity to take a growth leap.

What Ten Dates for Mates *is not*

Ten Dates for Mates is not:
—for marriages in deep trouble.
—for a wife or husband to work through alone.
—for passive reading.

What is included?

The ten dates have two strategic parts:

1. *Preparation time* (approximately one hour per date). This includes reading a short chapter and answering initial questions.

2. *The actual date* (one evening or afternoon). In a relaxed atmosphere of a date setting (away from phone, children, dogs, and interruptions), the couple works through a short project that helps them put principles into immediate practical application.

Why another book on marriage?

We go to the dentist every six months (or we should!) for a checkup. Our goal is to avoid major dental problems by having small cavities filled before they get bigger. *Ten Dates for Mates* is an opportunity for a marital checkup, a chance to fill those small cracks and cavities and to prevent larger ones by fine-tuning, enriching, and deepening the marital relationship.

Why is Ten Dates for Mates unique?

1. *It is short and concise.* The key to success is actually taking the time to work through a program, and a couple is more likely to do that if the program is not too long and overwhelming. Therefore, we have kept it short and to the point. It is better to discuss together one simple concept than to get partway through fifty steps to a better marriage.

2. *It is practically oriented.* *Ten Dates for Mates* deals with our marriages right where they are.

3. *The couple is actively involved.* The projects are designed to involve couples in a deeper level together.

4. *It is a track to run on, but not a straitjacket!* A step-by-step outline is provided, including:

—where to go
—what to do
—time commitment

If the material is too structured for you, take the ideas you like and structure it yourself. Or perhaps you want to be guided through the mechanics so you can give full attention to growing together in your relationship.

5. *It is fun* . . . because it is simple and does not require hours of study and preparation. The dates have enough structure to encourage communication, but not so much that they become work.

What will it cost me in time?

Preparation time for each date will be around one hour. For the actual dates we suggest:
1. One evening a week for ten weeks. If this is impossible, then consider . . .
2. One evening every two weeks for twenty weeks, or
3. One evening each month for ten months, or
4. Take a whole week or weekend away (just the two of you) to put romance into your relationship! The key is *planning* and *doing*!

Will it really make a difference?

It will be helpful only if used. The difference between reading a book and having your marriage enriched is your response—in one word: *involvement*! Our goal is to help you enrich and deepen your marital relationship, to learn new and better ways to relate to each other.

Statistics show that it takes three weeks to break or start a habit and six weeks to feel good about it. We suggest ten weeks of dates to grow in intimacy and actively work on your relationship. Perhaps your date night will become a new habit and you will benefit from the experience long past the initial ten dates!

I'm convinced! How can I start?

1. The first step is to decide together to *commit yourselves* to the ten dates. (See special notes to husbands and to wives on tips for presenting the idea.) It really doesn't matter *who* found the book and whose idea it was. The important thing is that both of you are willing to commit yourselves to having ten dates together to enrich your relationship.

2. The second step is to get out the planning calendar and *write in ten dates*! We

suggest one night a week—for example, every Thursday night at seven. Select an evening when you are less likely to have other commitments.

3. Make special arrangements to clear your schedule.
   a. Arrange baby-sitters.
   b. Plan meals ahead for the children.
   c. Plan your schedule light on that day to avoid fatigue.

4. What about interruptions, such as sick children and other unexpected problems? We all know that despite the best planning, there are times when plans have to be altered and changed. When this happens on your date night, reschedule it for the same week, if possible, and persevere. This takes commitment, so hang in there and guard your time together like a hawk!

One couple decided to take a whole weekend away to go through *Ten Dates for Mates*. Only after much perseverance did it really happen. The first time, the wife arranged for a sitter, cooked the food, cleaned the house—and at the last minute the chicken pox came to visit. The second time, she again got the sitter, cooked the food, cleaned the house—and this time the sitter got sick! Finally, the third time, it worked.

Her comment after the weekend away: "What a wonderful time we had together. I'm so glad we kept trying—it was well worth the hassle of cooking fifteen meals and cleaning the house three different times in order to have the time away with my husband. I've already started freezing meals for the next time!"

5. Each week, anticipate your date with your mate. Think of ways to let your spouse know you're looking forward to being with him or her. Don't rule out special surprises like phone calls and notes to express a positive attitude to your mate.

6. Sometime before each date, study through the short chapter you will be discussing and fill out the project for the corresponding date. (That should not take more than an hour.) Each chapter gives practical suggestions for preparation and participation. It would be helpful for each spouse to have his or her own copy of *Ten Dates for Mates*.

7. Follow the guide on each date, and do *not* use date time to deal with other issues and problems.

8. Don't forget the importance of eye contact. Remember, too, it's hard to be negative when you're holding hands with your mate.

9. Get started and have fun!

DATE ONE

Purposes: 1. To verbalize some positive thoughts about my mate to my mate, thus starting our dating on a positive note.

                  2. To better comprehend three basic principles of a successful marriage:
                      a. Leaving (Breaking away)
                      b. Cleaving (Commitment)
                      c. Becoming one flesh (Oneness)

Time Commitment: One evening, and one hour of preparation.

Preparation:

      BOTH: Read Chapter 1: "The High Priority Marriage." Answer the questions in Project 1 at the end of the chapter.

  HUSBAND: Make reservations at a favorite restaurant. (You may want to let the place be a surprise.)

      WIFE: Make arrangements for the children. Get a baby-sitter if needed. This could be set up on a regular weekly basis for ten weeks. Wives, plan what you will wear, choose an outfit you think your husband likes. Remember, this is a *date*!

THE HIGH PRIORITY MARRIAGE

The Arps are among that species in the Western world known as "tennis buffs." That doesn't mean we are super players, but we have managed to win our share of matches. Sometimes we even smash the experts. What's our secret? We've learned to play as a team.

Bob and Marie each rate in the expert category, but when we play doubles against them we usually win. How can that be? Individually they make some excellent shots, but the word *teamwork* isn't in their vocabulary. They compete not only with their opponents, but with each other too. And the person who messes up a shot really hears about it! In essence, they are two people playing singles on the same side of the net.

Although we make our share of bad shots and blunders, we minimize our errors through good communication. We've studied our strengths and weaknesses; we know who is good at the net and when one of us should play back. We've spent time working out our strategy. We don't win all of the time, but when we lose we're still pulling together (except on those days when we blow it too!). But over the long haul we've learned to work together, and we enjoy teaming up for tennis.

In many ways marriage is like playing doubles in tennis. Teaming up leads to success. You want to be partners instead of opponents. During the following ten dates we want to help you improve your teamwork—to get your strategy down and to experience ten weeks of training to help you be a winning team.

Marriage is a partnership

Our goal in marriage is to be a winning team. This involves both partners' willingness to share the load, to build a partnership. One wife expressed her desires and frustrations this way:

What we really need in our marriage is to be a team and to work together—not just being in the same house or room together, but to really talk and to share our feelings. Oh, we talk, but it's just about surface issues—my husband's job, the children, or what we're eating for dinner. We don't really share ourselves with each other. We each seem to have a protective wall. I take care of the home and the children; at times I feel like the maid. I feel isolated and cut off. Why can't our marriage be different? Why can't we talk? I'm willing to try, but I don't know anything I can do that will make a difference.

Perhaps you can identify with some of the feelings expressed by this wife, or with the frustration felt by her husband when she asked for a divorce.

Marriage is never static; it's always changing. Your marriage is either growing or withering.

Where are you?

Where are you in your marriage today? Perhaps you already have a winning team and you're looking for new ways to improve your plays and keep on winning. Or perhaps your team is in a rut—you win some, you lose some, but you're not seeing much progress. Maybe your team just can't get it together at all; you're losing all the games and you want to get turned around. Wherever you are, we want to help you become a winning team, not two separate players striving alone to win the game of marriage.

Married but alone?

When was the last time you felt alone in your marriage? It is possible to be married and still be very alone—to be physically close but emotionally miles away. Dave recalls:

When we made our first major move back in 1973, we experienced all kinds of difficulties and our own communication with each other began to slip. I was all wrapped up in my new job, and the challenges to me were a real adventure. Not so with Claudia, who missed her home, friends, and had to continually keep up with three little boys, ages fifteen months, four, and six years old, who had their own set of frustrations that they dumped on her. To say nothing of having no home for three months!

We were very close physically, especially when we were living in our VW camper! But emotionally, Claudia felt alone. Had I known then what we are sharing with you in *Ten Dates for Mates,* our first summer in Europe could have been quite different. But in actuality we were alone, and we can say from experience . . . it is not good.

What is aloneness?

Aloneness can be many things in a marriage. In our situation it was an *emotional isolation.*

Claudia says, "I felt emotionally isolated from Dave. He didn't understand where I was emotionally, and communication was blocked. Dave was being fulfilled in his new job but was not aware of my emotional needs."

Aloneness can be an *intellectual difference.* Have you ever heard the statement, "We've just grown apart. We don't seem to have anything in common anymore." This brings us to *lack of shared experiences.* One wife put it this way: "My husband finds time for everything and everyone else—why not for me?"

Aloneness can also be *physical incompatibility.* The sexual relationship may be either a battleground or a dull routine experience. Perhaps there is an *inability to stand together against trials.* It's each one for himself—the old "you handle your problems and I'll handle mine." However it is experienced, it's not good to be alone.

A *winning combination*

So where can we find a realistic game plan for marriage? Dave relates:

Some time ago I was making color slides to use with the seminar. After hours of setting up the material to be used and making the 108 slides, I drove across town to the Kodak laboratory to get them developed overnight. The next morning I picked up my 108 masterpieces. As I opened the first box I found 36 black slides; I opened the second box—you guessed it—36 more black slides followed by 36 black slides in the third box! What did Kodak do to my slides? Nothing! I checked my camera and all was okay as far as I could tell.

Lastly, I got out the instruction manual. Would you believe that one little button on the side of the camera was in the wrong position? One button set wrong gave me 108 black slides and hours of lost time. Had I read the instruction manual first, I could have avoided all this pain and misery, not to mention the cost in dollars. The camera manufacturers designed and engineered my camera. They know how it is designed to work and how it will work best. All I had to do was to read and follow their instruction.

Who created marriage?

God created and designed marriage, and He didn't do it in a vacuum or in the dark. He gave us a detailed instruction manual describing how it is designed to work. If we are willing to follow His instructions, we can get the most out of our marriages. But only if we start with the right premise can we come to the right conclusion. So let's start with the first marriage manual ever written—the Bible.

Biblical principles for relationships work. In this chapter we want to consider three principles for marriage found in the Scriptures. Ignore any one of them and you're in for "black slides" in your marriage. Follow all three and you'll have a clear, sharp picture of what a fulfilling marriage relationship can be.

THREE PRINCIPLES FOR SUCCESS

In Genesis 2:24 we read: "For this cause a man shall leave his father and his mother, and shall cleave to his wife; and they shall become one flesh."

Immediately after God created Eve, He gave these basic instructions on marriage. He knew the potential problems! Here we see three principles basic to any successful marriage: (1) *leaving,* (2) *cleaving,* and (3) *becoming one flesh.*

The commitment to leave

"For this cause a man shall leave his father and his mother." Leaving is a physical act, but it is also an attitude. Many people enter marriage willing to run home to mother at the first crisis; they have difficulty cutting the emotional apron strings.

My husband and I didn't get along well at all in the first months of our marriage. We were living in another town and I remember calling my mother. We had had a ghastly fight and I wanted to come home. My mom refused to let me come (wise mother!). She told me, "You married him; you've just got to work it out."

This wife was in the process of learning to leave. Running home to mama was not an option—she had to learn alone with her husband how to work things out. We are never to stop honoring our parents, but we are to leave them.

The principle of leaving involves refocusing our lives on each other—looking to each other to meet our emotional needs and not to others, be they parents or friends. It also involves giving other relationships and things a lesser priority than our relationship with our mate. Dr. Ed Wheat, in his practical book *Love Life for Every Married Couple,* shares this observation from his twenty-five years of counseling: "When a man consistently puts his business or career ahead of his wife, nothing he can buy with money will really please her."[1]

Is there an area in your life that you still need to leave—an area you need to give a lower priority than your relationship with your mate? What about your job? Or have you designated a higher priority to your children than to your spouse? What about your hobbies, or friends, or television? Are you over-involved in community service activities or even too committed to church activities? We knew one wife who had a different church meeting to attend every night of the week! Perhaps keeping a neat home and polished silver is too important to you. Unless we are willing to leave all else—counting other people and activities less important than our mates—we will not experience the oneness that is protection against aloneness.

The commitment to cleave

"And shall cleave to his wife."

What does it mean to cleave to one's mate? Webster's defines cleaving as "to adhere; to cling; to stick; to be faithful to." Another definition we have read is "to cement together." The principle of cleaving is one of commitment and permanence. To cast in concrete is to permanently cleave.

There is no six-months trial, money-back guarantee on marriage! As one couple commented when they were following the Cleave Principle during a rather difficult time in their marriage, "We had made a commitment to stick together—divorce was not an option—so for us it was either murder or suicide!" Without this kind of total commitment to our mates, how easy it would be to give up when problems come along (and those of us who have been married more than two weeks know that problems are a given factor in any marriage).

We all have daily opportunities to apply the Cleave Principle to our marriage relationships. The daily pressures of life, the hard times as well as the good times, can help to cement us together. The key is to pull together instead of pulling apart. Are you loyal and committed to your mate? Do you give your marriage team faithful support?

Let's get specific. What type of things tend to pull you together? These are positive, so don't try to avoid them. What things tend to tear you apart? These are negative situations; avoid them as much as possible. When you have a choice to make, ask yourself, "Will this action or attitude bring us closer together or will it put distance in our relationship?" When we have left our childhood homes and are cleaving to our mates, we have the wonderful opportunity to truly become one.

The commitment to oneness

"And they shall become one flesh."

Not only are we to leave and to cleave, but we are to become one flesh—growing in intimacy in all areas, enjoying one another completely. In God's sight, marriage means to become one. This is one reason why divorce is so devastating: the result is not two people going their own separate ways, but two parts of one. What a fragmented life and a picture of incompleteness! Let's choose to be our mate's completer.

Oneness means that the husband and wife are on the same team. If one loses the game, both lose. There can be no winner unless both win. Any help we offer our mates helps our team. Any pain, hurt, insult, any lack of support or faithfulness, any failure to help our mates reflects back on our team. We can be the most reinforcing human agent in our mates' lives and they in ours if we are willing to follow these three principles of leaving, cleaving, and becoming one flesh.

Marriage is a process. Like a soccer game, there are no time-outs. Marriages are constantly changing—withering or growing.

It's your turn!

We encourage you to begin your ten dates by reviewing your own commitment to these three principles. Begin positively. It's easy to see our mates' faults rather than their positive qualities.

Remember that one of the purposes of Date 1 is to verbalize some positive thoughts about your mate to your mate, thus beginning your dating on a positive note. So as you talk through the questions, be determined to stay positive. If negative areas show their ugly faces, make a note of them and save them for another time. Now, relax and enjoy the opportunity to spend time alone with your mate—and don't forget to have fun!

---

1. Ed Wheat, *Love Life for Every Married Couple* (Grand Rapids, Mich.: Zondervan, 1980), p. 28.

PROJECT
THE HIGH PRIORITY MARRIAGE

1. Think about why you chose to leave your own family and to cleave to your wife.

    A. List three things that attracted you to your wife.

        1.

        2.

        3.

    B. What do you think attracted your wife to you?

        1.

        2.

        3.

2. What types of things tend to draw you together?

3. What types of things tend to pull you apart?

15

PROJECT
THE HIGH PRIORITY MARRIAGE

1. Think about why you chose to leave your own family and to cleave to your husband. *desire for own home, own children, etc.*

   A. List three things that attracted you to your husband.
      1. *Caring, friendliness*
      2. *Well-organized – able to get things done*
      3. *Handsome.*

   B. What do you think attracted your husband to you?
      1. *People seemed to like me.*
      2. *Ambition*
      3. *Physical attractiveness*

2. What types of things tend to draw you together?
   Concerns over family
   Working together on projects of mutual benefit. Time with family

3. What types of things tend to pull you apart?
   Money concerns due to different priorities. Retirement plans not entirely met. New car vs. new drapes. New pool vs. education fund for future. When one of us devotes time looking for property or looking after property. Spending all of our time on work around house – not enough time to play – tennis, golf, etc. Work schedule.

DATE ONE

DATE NIGHT

Plan to use the whole evening (don't plan to rush home for your favorite TV program!). During a leisurely dinner discuss the three questions in Project 1. Allow enough time for talking.

Question 1—Husband goes first and reads what he has written down beforehand. Then wife answers question 1.

Question 2—Wife shares her answer first. Then husband shares.

Question 3—Husband first, then wife.

IMPORTANT: *Stay on the positive. If conflicts arise in the conversation, note and save for later, but don't discuss now.*

ASSIGNMENT

Look for ways to compliment each other this week. Try to give at least one honest compliment each day. Read Chapter 2.

EXTRA READING FOR THE EAGER BEAVER

Getz, Gene. *The Measure of a Marriage.* Glendale, Calif.: Regal, 1980.

Meredith, Don. *Becoming One.* Nashville: Thomas Nelson, 1979.

Wheat, Ed. *Love Life for Every Married Couple.* Grand Rapids, Mich.: Zondervan, 1980.

DATE TWO

Purposes: 1. To reexamine my expectations for marriage, both before we were married and now.
2. To better understand my mate's expectations.

Time Commitment: One evening, and one hour of preparation.

Preparation:

BOTH: Read Chapter 2: "Great Expectations."
Separately fill out Expectation Survey.

GREAT EXPECTATIONS

Let's meet Mark and Paula.

Mark grew up as a very self-sufficient only child. He had always been able to entertain himself and especially enjoyed his hobby—sports cars. He never had many deep friendships—that was, until he met Paula. After a brief courtship, they married and began their life together.

Paula was from a large, close-knit family, and she desired that her relationship with Mark would always be close. During their first years of marriage she resented his weekly night out with the boys. It seemed that Mark's time was always filled with his own activities, especially rebuilding sports cars. How she wished he would spend more of his time with her and that they could have some hobbies together!

Children came and Mark, for the most part, left it up to Paula to rear them. She often complained, and she couldn't understand why Mark was not more involved with his own family. Mark didn't understand why Paula wasn't happy; wasn't he a good provider for her? Why did she continually nag him about his private life and activities?

Paula desired a more intimate relationship with Mark, who wanted a life of his own apart from the marriage relationship. Both Mark and Paula need to identify their expectations of marriage. Only then will they be able to work out a compromise.

Expectations—what do you want?

What expectations did you bring into your marriage? Have they been met? What expectations do you have today? Listen to what others have said:

The main reason I got married was for sex.

I wanted my husband to make lots of money so he could buy me nice things.

I expected him to spend time with the family—that's important to me.

I wanted a wife to meet my needs—someone who would be a lot like me.

What was really important to me in my marriage was to have peace and harmony. To know that when we went to bed at night everything was okay.

I wanted a wife who was pretty and physically stacked. Someone who would take care of my needs and keep the house and my clothes clean.

What I wanted in marriage was romance!

I was looking for security and love and someone I could trust and lean on.

I wanted my husband to be my strength and to take care of me.

Before marriage, I had my mother to take care of my needs. After marriage, I expected my wife to do that.

Obviously, some of these couples were in for some shocks when their mates were unable to live up to their expectations. Dr. Selma Miller, president of the Association of Marriage and Family Counselors, states: "The most common cause of marriage problems is that partners' needs are in conflict, but they can't discuss the conflict because they don't know one exists. They only know they are miserable."[1]

●

Involvement—how much?

Do you approach marriage more from Paula's perspective or from Mark's? How much involvement do you desire to have with your mate? How much do you desire intimacy, closeness, and the deep sharing of life's experiences with your mate? Sharing life deeply with one another and being loved, trusted, and appreciated even when the other understands our weaknesses gives us a sense of identity and self-confidence in our marriage relationship. The accompanying diagram illustrates different degrees of involvement between marriage partners.[2]

DEGREES OF INVOLVEMENT IN MARRIAGE

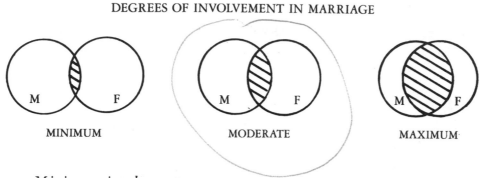

Minimum involvement

In a minimum involvement marriage, the lives of the husband and wife overlap very little. They go in different directions and meet only occasionally. They have separate interests and hobbies and are usually quite independent of each other. The wife is not irritated or bothered if the husband is often away on business. He is not really missed!

"I keep forgetting my husband is out of town," said an acquaintance of ours who has this style of marriage. We used to question the stability and success of their marriage, wondering why they did not experience more tension since they spent very little time together. Once the wife commented, "If my husband died, my life really wouldn't change." We were astounded! Why? Because for us that sort of distance would be unthinkable. Our style of marriage is different from theirs.

Maximum involvement

We have chosen a maximum involvement marriage style; our lives are very involved with each other. We do seminars together, we write together, we enjoy sports together. We make most decisions together and share deeply with each other our innermost thoughts and dreams. Our circles overlap to a great extent, although we still have interests and activities that do not include the other.

So it is easy to look at our friends who have chosen a minimum involvement style of marriage and question it. But if both partners agree about the amount of involvement desired with the other, then we should not consider their marriage unsuccessful.

Moderate involvement

Several years ago, before we began working closely together, Dave was with IBM. At that time in our marriage we were close in many areas, but not in the area of Dave's occupation. Claudia knew little about computer technology, and Dave's job required traveling. Even though we shared our feelings, dreams, and ambitions, our lives together were not as involved as they are today. Our marriage at that time in our lives was one of moderate involvement.

Let's consider another couple we know whose marital circles overlap about halfway. The husband is involved in a business that requires some travel. His wife, though supportive, is not involved in his work. She has her activities or job during the day and is involved in several civic clubs. They have a good social life together, and they enjoy mutual friends. They are both satisfied with each other and with the involvement level in their marriage.

All three marriage styles can be successful. And in between these three styles is a whole range of varying shades and degrees of involvement. Where would you place your marriage? With which circle do you identify the most? Which degree of involvement would your mate choose?

The key is that both partners are satisfied and agree on the amount of involvement with each other in their marriage. Problems develop when the involvement expectations of the husband and that of the wife are not the same. Watch out—sparks will fly!

Areas of expectations

It's important that we identify and decide on the degree of involvement we want, but we also need to look at other areas of expectations in marriage. It's hard enough to meet expectations when we know what they are, but it is almost impossible when we don't know what our mate expects.

Consider the couple whose marriage exploded after fifteen years. The husband had wanted his wife to replace his best pal that he had lost in the war, and the wife had wanted her husband to love and baby her as her dad used to do. Needless to say, they did not fulfill each other's expectations; they didn't even realize what they were!

What are your expectations? Why did you get married? What is most important to you and to your mate?

Let's look at seven areas of expectations in marriage. After each has been explained, you will be asked to rank them in order of their importance to you in your marriage.

1. *Security*—The knowledge of permanence in the relationship and of financial and material well-being.

2. *Companionship*—Having a friend who goes through all the joys and sorrows of life with you, a soul partner; also having some common (enjoyable) areas of interest and activity that you do together.

3. *Sex*—The oneness that comes through physical intimacy in marriage; the initiation and enjoyment of a growing physical relationship.

4. *Understanding and tenderness*—Experiencing regularly the touch, the kiss, the wink across the room that says, "I love you," "I care," "I'm thinking of you."

5. *Encouragement*—Having someone verbally support and appreciate your work and efforts in your profession, with the children, in providing financial security, running a household, and so on.

6. *Intellectual closeness*—Discussing and growing together in common areas of intellectual thought.

7. *Mutual activity*—Doing things together—politics, sports, church work, hobbies.

Now fill out the Expectation Survey.[3] Be prepared for some surprises, and remember that this is valuable information that can be used to enrich your relationship. Enjoy your date!

1. Mary Susan Miller, "What Are Your Expectations from Marriage?", *Family Life Today*, October, 1980, p. 19.

2. David and Vera Mace, *We Can Have Better Marriages if We Really Want Them* (Nashville: Abingdon, 1974), p. 76.

3. Miller, *Family Life Today*, p. 19.

PROJECT
GREAT EXPECTATIONS

1. Rank in order of 1 to 7 what is most important to you in your marriage (1 is highest; 7 is the lowest).
2. Rank in order of 1 to 7 what you think is most important to your wife in your marriage.

MARRIAGE EXPECTATIONS

Husband		Wife
7	SECURITY	7
2	COMPANIONSHIP (friendship)	4
5	SEX	5
3	UNDERSTANDING AND TENDERNESS	1
4	ENCOURAGEMENT	6
6	INTELLECTUAL CLOSENESS	3
1	MUTUAL ACTIVITY	2

PROJECT
GREAT EXPECTATIONS

1. Rank in order of 1 to 7 what is most important to you in your marriage (1 is highest; 7 is the lowest).
2. Rank in order of 1 to 7 what you think is most important to your husband in your marriage.

MARRIAGE EXPECTATIONS

Husband		Wife
	SECURITY	
	COMPANIONSHIP (friendship)	
	SEX	
	UNDERSTANDING AND TENDERNESS	
	ENCOURAGEMENT	
	INTELLECTUAL CLOSENESS	
	MUTUAL ACTIVITY	

DATE TWO

DATE NIGHT

Go to your favorite coffee shop for dessert (or out to dinner if you feel rich!).
Identify the degree of involvement you now have in your marriage.

Are you both satisfied?

Is compromise needed? If so, don't despair. Help is coming in the following dates. Don't discuss further. Next week's date deals with getting on the same team. WARNING: *You may be tempted to react to new insights and expectations, but don't! The first step in enriching your marriage is to understand where you are now.*

Discuss and compare the Expectation Survey.

ASSIGNMENT

Take the area your spouse rated as the most important expectation and do something positive and practical in that area this week. For example, if your spouse valued companionship highest, make plans to spend extra time doing something fun together or doing something together that needs to be done, like grocery shopping or painting a room. If your spouse valued sex highest, make plans to fulfill some wish or desire this week, or initiate the lovemaking.

Read Chapter 3.

EXTRA READING FOR THE EAGER BEAVER

Mace, David and Vera Mace. *We Can Have Better Marriages If We Really Want Them.* Nashville: Abingdon, 1974.

Wright, Norman. *The Pillars of Marriage.* Glendale, Calif.: Regal, 1979.

DATE THREE

Purposes: 1. To better understand the basic differences in people.
2. To understand my mate's strengths and weaknesses and to see how we fit together as a team.
3. To deal with my past wrong responses toward my mate and ask for forgiveness if needed.

Time Commitment: One evening, and one to two hours of preparation.

If more time is needed for the project, then split it up and have two date nights instead of one.

Preparation:

BOTH: Read Chapter 3: "Unity in Diversity."
After reading the chapter *separately,* follow the steps under "Log Removal," *before the date.*
Part 1 is just between you and God—*do not share with your mate.*
Fill out Part 2 on strengths and weaknesses and be prepared to share with your mate.

UNITY IN DIVERSITY

It is amazing how two people can live together for many years and yet look at life from such different perspectives. Consider our friends who recently wrote us about their trip to Europe.

In thinking of writing about our trip, I read over Ed's notes and thought we would combine our diaries, but now I wonder if we made the SAME trip. He remembers how far it is from Stockholm to wherever, what the money exchange was, what we had for breakfasts, how many meals were on our own, and the address of every airline office in the four countries. It is really a truism that opposites attract and that God puts different people together in order to bring out the best? worst? in them. So if you want to know how far north or south we went, ask him. I have no idea! The nearest we ever came to divorce was once when we were going to New York by car—he was driving and I was the co-pilot (the only time!). I had the map upside down and we were going merrily south when he wanted to go north.

Do you ever wonder if you're on the same trip as your mate? It is obvious that not only do we all have different expectations in marriage, but we all are different people with different personalities. Let's consider two ways that people differ:
1. Basic approach to life—more facts-oriented or feelings-oriented?
2. Temperament—more introverted or extroverted?

OUR BASIC APPROACH TO LIFE

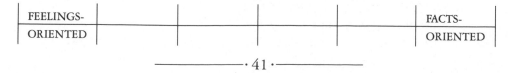

FEELINGS-ORIENTED					FACTS-ORIENTED

Feelings-oriented person

Consider the accompanying graph, which diagrams one of many human polarities.[1] On the left side we find the person who approaches life from a feelings orientation. When he speaks, he tends to express his feelings and emotions. He likes an open atmosphere in his marriage, and if tension is present in the relationship he strives to clear the air. His desire is to work through conflict and "not let the sun go down on his anger." It is important for him to have feedback from his mate. He is more relationship-oriented than a facts-oriented person.

Facts-oriented person

The person on the right side approaches life from a more cognitive orientation. He speaks to express ideas and to communicate information more than to express his feelings and emotions. He would rather not face unpleasant feelings and even becomes uncomfortable when emotional subjects are brought up. He prefers a peaceful coexistence rather than being confronted with emotions. He has a theoretical mind and is more goal-oriented than people-oriented. He tends to think in general ideas and is comfortable with subjects like his job, sports, and current events.

Our friend Ed tends to be facts-oriented. He recalls the events of the trip while his wife, being more feelings-oriented, is amazed at the facts he remembers.

Let's consider another couple we know. Phil is president of a computer company. He is very competent, successful, and a good provider for his family. He is comfortable in a world of facts and figures where emotional matters do not play a significant role, but he is less secure at home.

> I wanted to be a success and make a lot of money and the way you do that is to spend a lot of time at work and a small amount of time at home. Besides, the less time I spent at home, the less I had to get involved. My wife wants to have these emotional confrontations. She wants to talk about her feelings and fears and that makes me uncomfortable, so the result is that I spend more time at work.

Let's look at things from his wife's perspective. Gail wants to share her feelings, concerns, and desires with her husband and to work through each frustration with him. "Phil is a success in his profession," she says, "but at home not only does he not meet my needs, he doesn't even understand them." She interprets his lack of feelings as rejection. Consequently, they are far from benefiting from each other's differences. They're not playing on the same team!

What we are NOT saying

Take note! We are not saying the following three things:

1. *We are not saying that being on one side of the chart is better than being on the other side.* A feelings-oriented person is not less intelligent, nor does a facts-oriented person have fewer feelings.

Both approaches have strengths and weaknesses, advantages and disadvantages. Which side you or your mate tend to be on is less important than understanding where you are and that people are different.

2. *We are not saying that men are cognitive and women are emotional.* In our marriage, we both tend to be somewhere in the middle, but generally Dave is more feelings-oriented than Claudia. He is the one who is more sentimental and romantic, while Claudia tends to organize the facts and move on!

3. *We are not saying that everyone is EITHER feelings-oriented OR facts-oriented.* Dave is more facts-oriented than Claudia in some areas of our marriage. For instance, when our children are being criticized, Claudia is definitely more feelings-oriented than Dave.

It is not so important whether we are alike or different in our approach to life or to a special situation. But it is helpful to recognize which approach we are coming from.

Unwilling or unable?

When we come from different perspectives it is easy to confuse the *willingness* to change with the *ability* to change. Gerald Dahl, in his book *Why Christian Marriages Are Breaking Up,* points this out clearly as he describes a German farm couple. The husband was facts-oriented and had little space in his life for feelings. Dr. Dahl describes one of their counseling sessions:

> During one of our sessions the wife told me that her husband never said, "I love you." She went on to say that she would like to have him do this, "just like the neighbor's husband tells his wife."

My logical question, of course, to the husband was, "Do you love your wife?"

I knew the challenge ahead of me when he replied "I'm here, ain't I?"

When I asked him if he would be willing to start telling her that he loved her, he replied, "I suppose I could. But the words tend to stick in my throat. I never heard my folks say it to each other, nor did anyone tell it to me when I was growing up."

As our session continued I learned that during the winter months, part of his daily routine was to get up before his wife every morning, put on the coffee, brush the snow from her car, and start the engine. Then when she was ready to leave for work, her car was nicely warmed. She had a factory job ten miles away, which helped out financially during the slim winter months.

"Do you enjoy getting up and doing this each morning?" I asked.

"I hate it!" was his immediate reply. "The only person in the world I would do that for is sitting right there," he said, pointing his finger at his wife. "I know she likes that done for her," he concluded.

At that very moment she and I simultaneously realized that that was his "I love you." He would have been *willing* to say the words, but he did not have the *ability* to convey it verbally as sincerely as he did with his actions.[2]

OUR UNIQUE TEMPERAMENTS

More *differences*

Not only are there basic differences in the area of feelings and facts, but we each have a special temperament. We agree with our friend who confirmed in her travel experience that "opposites attract." However, those very characteristics that attracted a man to his wife—her easygoing nature, never in a hurry, always has time for people—may later be an irritation as it affects the efficiency of running a household.

A number of years ago when we left IBM and joined the staff of a Christian organization, we were required to take a battery of psychological tests. Until this time we had little confidence in such tests. Then we were interviewed by a Christian psychologist. As we sat in his office he said, "Now Dave, here are your strong points."

As he listed them Dave began to feel better and better. He went on, "Now here are the areas in which you are weak." That wasn't nearly as enjoyable for Dave to hear, but the psychologist was right on target!

Then he went through the same procedure with Claudia, listing her strengths and weaknesses. Looking at both of us, he said, "Dave and Claudia, here are the areas you agree upon, and here are the areas in which you tend to have problems." He could have been a fly on our walls the past year—he didn't miss anything! Our respect for those psychological tests went up about three hundred percent.

Then he gave Dave one of the most beneficial challenges of his whole life: "You probably noticed that your weak areas are Claudia's strengths and that Claudia's weak areas are your strengths. Now the challenge to you, Dave, is to let Claudia operate in her areas of strengths and not be threatened by her abilities in these areas. You have the potential for being a terrific team together."

Twelve years later

That was twelve years ago. Since that time we have learned to concentrate on the other's strengths and to really benefit from each other. It hasn't always been easy. It's hard to openly admit that your weakness is your mate's strength and vice versa.

We send out a newsletter regularly and this used to be a real point of frustration and conflict. Writing is not one of Dave's favorite things, so after days and weeks of Claudia's gentle and not-so-gentle prodding, Dave would sit down to write. Once he started writing, he would go on and on, ending up with a newsletter crowded with facts and details, pages too long.

When the first draft of the letter was finally finished, Dave, having a real sense of accomplishment, would show it to Claudia. She gave her opinion freely: "It's much too long. Why did you include this part? Cut this part out. Here, I'll help you." At that point, the only help Dave wanted was to be left alone. He knew Claudia was gifted in writing, but he was too threatened to benefit from her strength.

Once we began to concentrate on our strengths, Dave began to give Claudia more opportunities to help with our newsletters. Together we plan out the main ideas. Sometimes Dave chooses the theme and main points. Then Claudia takes it from there and puts it down on paper. She has even involved the boys and now they help with the art work. The results? Our newsletters are improving, Claudia is more fulfilled, and Dave is benefiting from Claudia's strengths. Over the years, Dave has learned how to better put down his thoughts on paper. It helps to concentrate on our areas of strength!

Several years ago, we retook the same psychological tests and had another conference with the same psychologist. The results confirmed that by allowing each other to operate in our areas of strengths, our weak areas were not as weak as before.

Pick your strengths

Study your own temperament and the temperament of your mate. Assess your strengths and weaknesses, and allow your mate to operate in his or her areas of strength as much as possible. For example, who keeps the financial records in your family, pays the bills, does the taxes? Claudia becomes very frustrated when it comes to finances. This is not her area of strength. Dave comes from an engineering background; here is one area where he can put all those math courses to work—so he handles the finances. This doesn't mean Claudia has nothing to say about our finances, or that she doesn't keep a record of checks she has written (at least *most* of the time!). But it does mean that Dave shoulders the responsibility in the area of finances.

Psychological tests are not required to determine your basic strengths and weaknesses and temperaments. In this chapter we will be going through a brief summary of the four basic temperaments. After you have determined what your own strengths and weaknesses are, then you can take up the challenge that was given to us years ago: Learn to let each other operate in his or her areas of strength instead of being threatened.

Four basic temperaments

The temperament theory was first conceived by Hippocrates more than twenty-four hundred years ago. It divides people into four basic categories. Extroverts are usually *sanguine* or *choleric* in temperament, while introverts are predominantly *melancholy* or *phlegmatic*. Generally, each of us is a combination of two or more of the temperaments, with one being dominant. Each temperament has its own set of strengths and weaknesses. By understanding our own temperament and that of our mate, we are better equipped to reach our potential in understanding each other. Understanding our strengths and weaknesses helps us work together as a team.

As we look briefly at the four basic temperaments, remember that no one could serve as an example of a pure temperament. We are all various blends. When we say someone has a choleric temperament, we don't mean that he is lacking in other traits, but simply that the choleric temperament is predominant in his personality.

We should never use the weaknesses of our temperament type to excuse ourselves. Have you heard others say, "Laziness is part of my personality—that's just the way I am"? We can study our temperaments to better understand how we respond to our surroundings, but we should never use them as an excuse for not working on an area of life that needs improvement!

Sammy Sanguine—No one can accuse Sam of not enjoying life. He lives life to the fullest and we always enjoy being with him. He makes us feel that we are the most important people in the whole world to him. Of course, when we are not with him he may forget all about us! He lives in the present. Sam is a true extrovert and loves to be with people. He is a great conversationalist, friendly, and responsive. He finds it very easy to apologize, which is good because he talks so much that he needs to apologize often! No one is more sincere, but after he makes promises he often forgets them.

Sam has been described as a butterfly who flutters from one flower to another; he leaves behind a whole line of unfinished jobs and projects. Many salesmen, actors, performers, and speakers are sanguines. They are warm and outgoing, compassionate and generous.

However, Sam tends to be weak-willed and undisciplined. He is the only friend we have who makes a new list of New Year's resolutions each month and who starts a new diet each week. He tends to be disorganized, which can lead to reduced productivity. In a group, Sam usually has the loudest voice; but face it, he really is a likeable guy! If you identify somewhat with Sam, let us give you a tip. Concentrate on working on the area of self-discipline and you can minimize your weaknesses.

Charlie Choleric—We just couldn't get along without our friend Action Charlie. With his great potential for activity he stimulates those around him. He has a will of iron and only has to make New Year's resolutions once every five years. Charlie is decisive and opinionated and great to have around in an emergency. He is very practical-minded and finds it easy to make decisions—not only for himself but for anyone around him. Productivity is his middle name and he has no lack of self-confidence, courage, and optimism. He too is an extrovert and a natural leader. Many of the world's great leaders have been from this temperament. Cholerics make good executives, idea people, dictators, or criminals—depending upon their moral standards.

If you are looking for sympathy, don't go to Charlie. He walks straight into a sensitive situation without even noticing, and he can be cold and inconsiderate to the others present. He can be stubborn and unyielding, so if Charlie is angry, watch out! When he oversteps his boundaries in relationships, it is very difficult for him to apologize. If you have choleric tendencies you have real potential, but to reach your potential you will need to control your temper and learn to apologize. Also, try not to be too domineering.

Marvin Melancholy—Now we turn to the introverted temperaments. Marvin Melancholy is the most faithful and dependable friend we could ever have. It took a while to get to know him, but loyalty is his byword. As with our sanguine friend, feelings predominate, but while Sammy demonstrates his feelings in an outward way Marvin tends to turn his feelings inward. This produces much introspection and self-centeredness. Although he is very sensitive and critical towards others, he is even harder on himself. He is never satisfied, for he is a perfectionist.

Where the sanguine is the enjoying temperament, Marvin is the suffering temperament. Melancholies make wonderful martyrs! He is a man of orderly habits and is very conscientious and self-disciplined. However, he tends to be idealistic. Marvin has a rich emotional life and usually likes the opera and fine arts. Many musicians, artists, doctors, and philosophers are melancholies.

Although highly gifted, Marvin has some liabilities. When he becomes moody and touchy, it's best to just remove yourself from his presence. He tends to take the most pessimistic view and can at times have a tendency toward revenge. It's hard for Marvin to compromise and hard for him to forget an insult. As one melancholy said, "I can forgive—I just can't forget!" Like the choleric, it is hard for him to apologize. To counteract the liabilities of this temperament, one needs to work against too much introspection and brooding.

Pete Phlegmatic—Pleasant Pete is the easiest person in the whole world to get along with, and probably the most likeable! He is always good-natured. We really like to have Pete around. Life for Pete is a fulfilling, pleasant, unexcited experience. Because his boiling point is so high, he seldom gets angry. He has a practical mind and is helpful to others in need.

Steady consistency describes our friend, Pete, but he is so s-l-o-w! If he doesn't counteract it, his slow pace can become laziness. He is a real diplomat and can be efficient and organized. He has the potential to be a good leader and a joy to follow.

On the minus side, Pete tends to be a spectator in life and at times can be blasé and unmotivated. He needs to work at overcoming his passivity. Our son Joel is a lovable phlegmatic. He is a delight to have as a son, but at times his easygoing disposition is a frustration, especially when lazy tendencies begin to appear. For his thirteenth birthday we gave him a challenge—to arise a few minutes earlier each morning and take a shower. This really helped him to learn self-discipline and to overcome being so passive.

The choleric looks at a situation and says, "The situation is critical, but not hopeless." The phlegmatic looks at the same situation and comments, "The situation is hopeless, but not critical!"

Suppose a letter of advice needed to be written. May we suggest the possible results:

—Sammy Sanguine, full of good intentions, never got around to writing.

—Marvin Melancholy didn't write because he knew it wouldn't do any good anyway.

—Charlie Choleric wrote, putting his advice in the format of an order.

—Pete Phlegmatic penned his advice like this: "I want to encourage you to consider the following . . ."

Personally applied

Most people are a combination of more than one of these temperaments. In our family, Dave is a phlegmatic with some sanguine. He is that easygoing guy, but a people-person, too. Isn't Claudia lucky? She could tell you, though, that he is easily sidetracked, rarely gets into overdrive, and needs God's Spirit to continually motivate him. Claudia is a combination of choleric and melancholy. There is not a phlegmatic cell in her whole body. Action is the key word, and if Dave doesn't plan his day Claudia will gladly do it for him!

Here is where a study of the temperaments has helped us. Dave explains:

I know that Claudia is an activist and needs opportunities to express herself, so I have encouraged her in her writing endeavors. The results are a book on children, written with friend Linda Dillow, called *Sanity in the Summertime*—and lots of excellent help in putting together our *Marriage Alive* Seminar and *Ten Dates for Mates*.

I have helped her channel her energy into directions that will benefit our team. I don't have to feel threatened on those days when Claudia is running on four cylinders as I'm trying to get my one cylinder started, because she is contributing to my team. What I don't want is Claudia competing against me!

Claudia comments:

By understanding Dave's temperament and mine, too, I can be a big help to Dave. Realizing that Dave's pace is slow but steady, I can encourage him by protecting him from interruptions, thus helping increase his productivity. I can allow God the Holy Spirit to be his motivator. He does a much better job than I used to do! I also can realize that my tendency is to organize those around me, of which Dave is one. This tendency is sometimes helpful with three boys, but I have to watch that manipulation does not become a part of our marital relationship.

Of course, neither of us has reached perfection in accepting each other's temperaments, but we're growing in this area and it is benefiting our team. Dave continues:

Sometimes I get frustrated because Claudia is so opinionated and particularly when she expresses a snap judgment as fact. She doesn't do this much with me anymore because I have learned to speak my mind and challenge her conclusions, but she still does it occasionally with our boys.

Recently, after much company, she was cleaning Jonathan's room and found a pair of her best gloves on his floor. Her quick mind assimilated the facts: The boys know they don't play with her good gloves; they were found in Jonathan's room; therefore he was guilty of taking the gloves and playing with them. She called Jonathan in for the sentencing without giving him a chance to explain or acknowledge if he was guilty or not. She did not take into consideration all the other children who had been playing in our home.

Later, I explained to Claudia what she had done. She had convicted Jonathan on pure circumstantial evidence without giving him the opportunity to reply. She saw my point. Claudia is learning not to make snap decisions and to listen to what I have to say from my perspective. There are times when we still feel threatened by each other. When Claudia is running on all eight cylinders and her mind is in its creative mode, she gets frustrated with me if I'm not on her wavelength and activity level . . . so we still have a way to go.

Our goal is not to be the same; we were created with these differences. But our goal is to accept each other and benefit from the strengths of each other. It takes work and a lot of patience, but it is one area in which we are growing.

Maybe this is an area you need to give some attention to in your marriage. We would like to give you some practical suggestions on how to begin.

"Log Removal"

What often happens when we see weaknesses in our mate is that we react negatively. That is the natural way, but God has a better way. In Matthew 7:3–5 we read:

> And why do you look at the speck in your brother's eye, but do not notice the log that is in your own eye? Or how can you say to your brother, "Let me take the speck out of your eye," and behold, the log is in your own eye? You hypocrite, first take the log out of your own eye, and then you will see clearly enough to take the speck out of your brother's eye.

Often we are so concerned with our mate's faults that we cannot see our own! We suggest the following exercise:[3]

Step 1—List your mate's faults and your wrong responses.
Make two columns on a sheet of paper. In the left-hand column, list all of your mate's faults. In the right-hand column, list your wrong responses to those faults. Perhaps your mate is always late. What is your response? Do you lecture, sigh, or start the silent treatment? As you do this exercise, you may find that your responses are as bad as or worse than the faults you've listed. After you have finished, confess your wrong attitudes to God and burn or tear up the paper. *Do not* show it to your spouse; this exercise is for your benefit to help you get the log out of your own eye!

Example:

FAULTS	WRONG RESPONSES
1. Never on time	1. Belittle
	2. Sigh or moan
	3. Nag
	4. Compare with others
	5. Criticize
	6. Neglect
	7. Reject as a person
	8. Cool sexually
	9. Anger
	10. Tear down
	11. Bitterness
	12. Silence

Step 2—Confess to God your wrong responses and attitudes.

In 1 John 1:9 we read: "If we confess our sins, He is faithful and righteous to forgive us our sins and to cleanse us from all unrighteousness." Remember, the emphasis here is on our wrong responses and attitudes, not on our mate's faults.

Step 3—Accept your mate with his or her temperament and corresponding strengths and weaknesses.

First Thessalonians 5:18 says: "In everything give thanks; for this is God's will for you in Christ Jesus." Have you ever thanked God for your mate's strengths and weaknesses? If not, do it now. God can use your mate's temperament to complete your own. It is impossible to change another person; the only people we can change are ourselves. When we concentrate on changing ourselves, on correcting our wrong responses and attitudes, wonderful things often happen. Others tend to change in response to us! So don't try to change your mate. Leave that to God, and concentrate on being the person your mate needs to complete his or her team. It is your job to make your mate happy and God's job to make him or her holy.

Step 4—Ask your mate's forgiveness for your past wrong responses.

Remember, no relationship can thrive without forgiveness. No marriage is perfect; we all blow it from time to time. Relationships are like potted plants: The pot can be broken, but if the plant is repotted and the roots are not left exposed, if it is watered and given tender loving care, it will continue to grow and thrive. Forgiveness is a vital part of marriage. Without it, relationships die—like the potted plant left with its roots exposed. So when your mate comes to you to ask you for forgiveness, give it! The director of a mental hospital said that half of his patients would be able to go home if they knew they were forgiven.

If you need to ask for forgiveness for your wrong responses and attitudes, do it the right way. Deal only with what you have done wrong, not with your mate's faults. For example: "Honey, I was wrong to nag you and to pout about being late to church. Will you forgive me?" NOT: "I'm sorry that I nagged you about being late to church, but you know you're wrong to always make us late!"

Remember that you are pointing the finger at what you have done wrong. Do not use asking for forgiveness as an opportunity to attack your mate, like the wife who said: "Because you are a harsh and uncompromising person I have found it hard to live with you and have failed to accept you. Will you forgive me?" Her husband would probably rather hit her than forgive her! How much better if she had said something like this: "I have come to realize that I have not been as loving and supporting of you as I should be. I want to be a different wife in the future. Will you forgive me?"

Step 5—Get on your mate's side!

Your mate does not need your help in pointing out his or her faults; there are plenty of people out there who will do that. You are the ones who need to build up each other. Remember, you can be the most positive reinforcement in your mate's life.

Your turn!

Take the time *now* to go through the five steps of Log Removal and deal with your own wrong responses. Do not share this with your mate, but do ask for forgiveness for any wrong responses or attitudes you have demonstrated. *Do Part 1 (Log Removal) in Project 3 before your date night.*

1. D. Ross Campbell, *How to Really Love Your Child* (Wheaton, Ill.: Victor, 1977), p. 20.

2. Gerald Dahl, *Why Christian Marriages Are Breaking Up* (Nashville: Thomas Nelson, 1979), pp. 75, 76.

3. Linda Dillow, *Creative Counterpart* (Nashville: Thomas Nelson, 1977), adapted from pp. 82–87. Used with permission of publisher.

4. Tim LaHaye, *Understanding the Male Temperament* (Old Tappan, N.J.: Revell, 1977), p. 56.

5. Ibid.

PROJECT
UNITY IN DIVERSITY

Part 1 (Log Removal) should be done before the date night.

Part 2—Understanding Your Strengths and Weaknesses.
    Use the diagram on the following page to assess your strengths and weaknesses and list them in the chart below. Do the same for your wife. (Fill out separately.)

My own		My wife's	
STRENGTHS	WEAKNESSES	STRENGTHS	WEAKNESSES

Use Figure 3 to assess your own strengths and weaknesses and those of your wife.[4]
Allow your wife to operate in her areas of strength *as much as possible*!

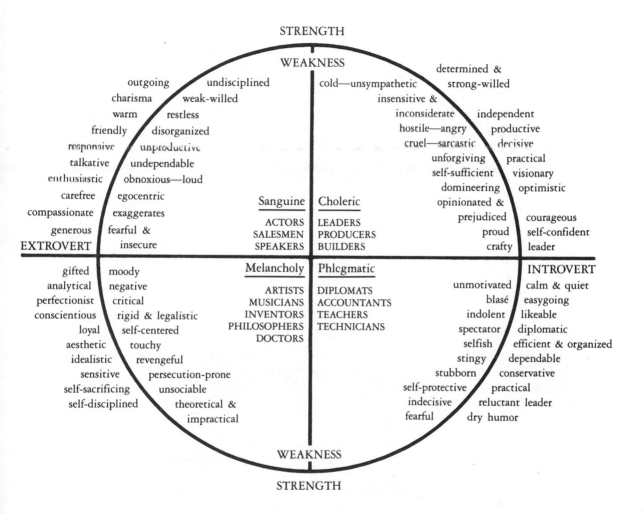

Fig. 3. THE FOUR BASIC TEMPERAMENTS

THEN COMPLETE THE FOLLOWING TOGETHER.

DISCUSS:

1. What are our strengths and weaknesses?
   (Make a conscious effort to concentrate mainly on the strengths—stay *positive*!)

2. List potential areas for complementing each other.

3. List potential areas for problems.

4. How can we benefit from our strengths?

PROJECT
UNITY IN DIVERSITY

Part 1 (Log Removal) should be done before the date night.

Part 2—Understanding Your Strengths and Weaknesses.

    Use the diagram on the following page to assess your strengths and weaknesses and list them in the chart below. Do the same for your husband. (Fill out separately.)

My own		**My husband's**	
STRENGTHS	WEAKNESSES	STRENGTHS	WEAKNESSES

Use Figure 3 to assess your own strengths and weaknesses and those of your husband.[5]
Allow your husband to operate in his areas of strength *as much as possible*!

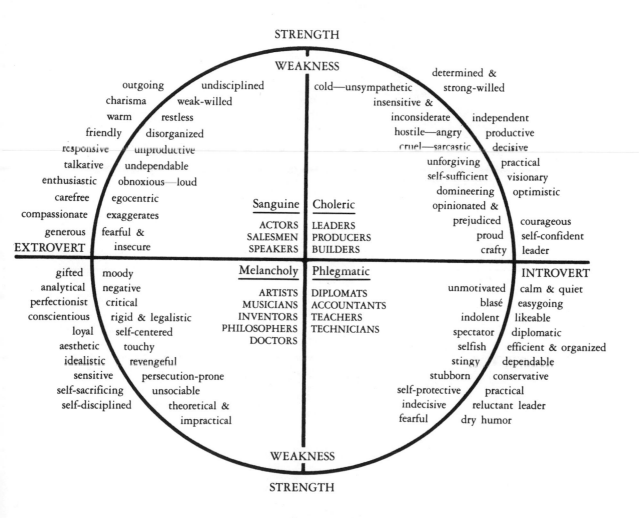

STRENGTH

WEAKNESS

outgoing	undisciplined	cold—unsympathetic	determined & strong-willed
charisma	weak-willed	insensitive & inconsiderate	
warm	restless		independent
friendly	disorganized	hostile—angry	productive
responsive	unproductive	cruel—sarcastic	decisive
talkative	undependable	unforgiving	practical
enthusiastic	obnoxious—loud	self-sufficient	visionary
carefree	egocentric	domineering	optimistic
compassionate	exaggerates	opinionated & prejudiced	
generous	fearful & insecure	proud	courageous / self-confident
		crafty	leader

Sanguine | Choleric

ACTORS | LEADERS
SALESMEN | PRODUCERS
SPEAKERS | BUILDERS

EXTROVERT

Melancholy | Phlegmatic

ARTISTS | DIPLOMATS
MUSICIANS | ACCOUNTANTS
INVENTORS | TEACHERS
PHILOSOPHERS | TECHNICIANS
DOCTORS |

INTROVERT

gifted	moody		unmotivated	calm & quiet
analytical	negative		blasé	easygoing
perfectionist	critical		indolent	likeable
conscientious	rigid & legalistic		spectator	diplomatic
loyal	self-centered		selfish	efficient & organized
aesthetic	touchy		stingy	dependable
idealistic	revengeful		stubborn	conservative
sensitive	persecution-prone		self-protective	practical
self-sacrificing	unsociable		indecisive	reluctant leader
self-disciplined	theoretical & impractical		fearful	dry humor

WEAKNESS

STRENGTH

Fig. 3. THE FOUR BASIC TEMPERAMENTS

THEN COMPLETE THE FOLLOWING TOGETHER.

DISCUSS:

1. What are our strengths and weaknesses?
   (Make a conscious effort to concentrate mainly on the strengths—stay *positive!*) *high standards conscientious understanding financial conservativeness grotto fun-loving sensitive loving humourous*

2. List potential areas for complementing each other.
   budget planning high standards pride in home cleanliness

3. List potential areas for problems.
   tardiness - lack of planning overscheduling - earlier start

4. How can we benefit from our strengths?

- Ask students to callback
- prioritize time & effort
-

DATE THREE

DATE NIGHT

Find a quiet and private location, like a friend's empty apartment, your office, or a quiet restaurant. If you go to a friend's apartment, take a picnic basket.

If you have not completed working through Part 1 (Log Removal), do so, but do it separately. *Do not share your list of faults and wrong responses with your mate!*

If necessary, ask for forgiveness for your wrong responses.

Then, if you have not already done so, fill out Part 2, Understanding Strengths and Weaknesses. When both are finished, discuss together, using the suggested questions. Summarize and write out your answers. *Remember to concentrate on strengths and stay positive!*

ASSIGNMENT

During the next week, write down the strengths that you see in your mate. Observe his or her personality traits. Think about how you can complement each other.

Is your mate strong in an area in which you are weak? How can this help your team?

Read Chapter 4.

EXTRA READING FOR THE EAGER BEAVER

Bright, Bill. *How to Experience God's Love and Forgiveness.* San Bernardino, Calif.: Campus Crusade, 1981.

Dillow, Linda. *Creative Counterpart.* Nashville: Thomas Nelson, 1977.

LaHaye, Tim. *The Spirit-Controlled Temperament.* Wheaton, Ill.: Tyndale, 1971.

Tournier, Paul. *To Understand Each Other.* Atlanta: John Knox, 1967.

DATE FOUR

Purposes: 1. To learn how to build up instead of tear down my mate.
2. To learn to break the negative thought pattern by learning to praise.

Time Commitment: One evening, and one hour of preparation.

Preparation:

BOTH: Read Chapter 4: "Building Each Other Up." *Separately* fill out questions in Project 4.

BUILDING EACH OTHER UP

Derrik and Karen had gone through an unbelievably hard time in their lives. They had been uprooted from their home and friends for several months. Add three small children, sickness, and other pressures, and our friends were about bankrupt emotionally. Time was definitely needed to get their act back together, so they planned a week away without the children.

As they drove away that morning, things looked bleak. Karen was tired and depressed; she felt like a failure. She just couldn't seem to get herself moving. After about an hour they stopped for lunch, and for the next thirty minutes her husband praised her. He didn't just list three or four things about her—it was more like thirty! Small areas, larger areas, insignificant things—on and on he went describing things he appreciated about her and her love. What a significant difference this thirty minutes made in her outlook on life!

Derrik later shared with us, "Those thirty minutes made such a difference in our whole week. It set the stage, and from the beginning of the week Karen knew that I loved, admired, and respected her."

Karen's postcard, written during their week together, tells of the happy results, the by-product of his praise: "It's amazing how things come into focus when we take the time to be alone. We've had so much fun, but now I'm ready to go home even though I still must face some unsolved problems."

The other side of the coin

What would have been the results if Derrik had said to Karen, "Honey, you've just got to get control of yourself. Cut out the tears! You're not coping and you're falling apart. Your attitude is having a negative effect on our children. If you tried harder, I know you could do better." The week would have been a first-class disaster and Karen would have been devastated! To tear down your mate is one of the most cruel and unloving things you can do; it spells defeat for your relationship.

Four to one for praise

It has been estimated that it takes four positive statements to offset one negative statement. Too often in marriage, the ratio of positive statements to negative statements is one to four, not four to one. How would you rate?

Our spouses desperately need us to build them up. If we don't, who will? Their bosses? Don't count on it. The children? How many children walk in and say, "Mom and Dad, I want to express my appreciation to you for your consistent discipline and for not letting me do certain things I want to do because you know they are not in my best interest." Ours never have! Will our friends build us up? If we're fortunate they might, but we can't count on it. Our mates need our encouragement! You can be the most positive reinforcing agent in your mate's life if you choose building up instead of tearing down.

But how does one begin? Let us give you three suggestions for building up your mate:

1. Concentrate on your mate's strengths.
2. Build self-esteem in your mate.
3. Learn to be a praiser.

Pushing the positive

The first thing we can do is to concentrate on each other's strengths. This does not come naturally. Consider this illustration:

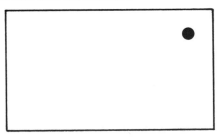

Where do our eyes immediately focus? On the small, dark spot. We ignore all the light area and see only the small dark spot. In the same way, we have a tendency to concentrate on our mate's faults and on his or her weak areas. Why? Could it be that our own insecurities are showing and we are trying to justify or hide our own weaknesses?

In our brief study of temperaments in the last chapter, the one thing that became clear is that all of us have both strengths and weaknesses. Strengths and weaknesses assure us neither of success nor of failure in our marriages. They are merely the setting or the field where we play our game of marriage. Remember our challenge to you to let your mate operate in his or her area of strength? When we choose not to be threatened by our mate's strengths, even in areas where we are weak, we learn from each other. Let's look at some practical examples.

Consider the following—what would be your response?

1. You are a wife whose husband is a stickler for organization. You can:
    a. not even try to be organized because you don't want to compete and lose. You already feel inferior in this area.
    b. criticize him for being too organized.
    c. appreciate his gift of organization and be sure to tell him, then learn from him in this area.
2. You are a husband who would love to be a hermit, but whose wife is a gifted conversationalist. You can:
    a. criticize your wife for being too talkative.
    b. send your wife as your representative to all social functions.
    c. appreciate her natural talent in this area, verbalize your appreciation, and benefit from her insights. Ask her for suggestions for conversation openers and other tips for keeping conversations rolling along.

Every day you make choices to build up or tear down, to benefit by your mate's strengths or to be threatened by them. Just be glad your mate brings his or her strengths to your team; what you don't want is competition!

Building self-esteem

There are basically three elements we must consider in building your own self-esteem and that of your mate. If any one of the three is missing, then how we view ourselves will be affected. The three elements are:

1. *Sense of worth*—knowing we are of value and are appreciated by others.

2. *Sense of belonging*—feeling a part of our world; knowing that we are loved and needed, that we're on a team.

3. *Sense of competence*—having the ability to do something well; having confidence in our own abilities.

Building self-worth—How can we build self-worth in our mates? Let's consider Bob and Susie.

Bob was having a rough week at the office. The regional boss was inspecting the whole operation and Bob felt personally responsible. The tension had spilled over into the home and he had not been easy to live with. Susie had a choice to make. She could let him know that she didn't appreciate his touchiness and insensitivity to her and to the children, or she could build him up. Being a wise woman, she chose the latter. During the week he found notes in his briefcase that said things like:

> "Inspections come and inspectors go;
> through it all I love you so!"

> "Integrity, honesty, sensitivity to me,
> Your many good qualities I do see."

> "When you get home, it may be late,
> but just remember, we have a date!"

What have you done this week to build self-worth in your mate? Stop and list three things you can do next week. Maybe jingles aren't your style, but find some way to say, "You are of great value to me and I appreciate you!" A note or phone call affirming your commitment to and belief in your mate can alter his or her day.

Building a sense of belonging—Dave relates:

Some of the closest times in our own marriage have been when things were rough on the outside. Before we began to work full-time in the area of marriage enrichment, we went through a long, hard year before getting the "go ahead" to proceed in this direction. The year included many meetings, proposals, deadlines, and delays. Many times we were weary and ready to give up. For each two steps forward we took, it seemed there were three steps back! I don't think we would have made it if Claudia had not been on my team, willing to encourage me when I was down. She had her down times too, but fortunately they were when I was up and could encourage her.

Does your mate know you're glad he or she is on your team? When have you told him or her so? If it hasn't been in the last week, get busy!

Building a sense of competence—Let's consider the last element of self-esteem—having a sense of competencey. Do you take pride in doing something well? Let us encourage you to choose one area and develop competence in it. Husband, you can encourage your wife to develop at least one interest outside the home. It will give her contact with other people and broaden her world. It will also help in the area of self-esteem.

Claudia shares:

Several years ago, Dave encouraged me to take tennis lessons. Sports was one area that was just not my "thing" and I always felt inferior around people who were athletic. Because many of my friends as well as Dave played tennis, I decided to give it a try. It wasn't that easy with three small boys, and it took some persistent planning and shuffling, but I'm so glad today that I did it! I'm not a fantastic player, but I can hold my own in most games. It has been a good outlet for me, a good form of exercise, and it has given me a real sense of accomplishment. No longer do I feel inferior around my athletic friends, and on the home front I now have four tennis partners instead of one. All three boys enjoy taking on Mom, and they don't always beat her!

Help your mate to develop competence in at least one area. Tennis may not be the right outlet, but find an area of interest and go for it. Be willing to encourage each other in this area.

One wife we know, in order to encourage her husband to continue with racquetball, invited other couples for dinner until he found a racquetball partner. (The other wife was also an encourager.) Then she called all over town and found court time for them and signed them up for a season spot. Smart gal! She knew her husband needed this outlet, but being work-oriented he probably would not have pursued it on his own.

Another friend of ours gave his wife a ten-week course in ceramics. Small children, limited finances, and an unlimited "to do" list had kept her from pursuing it. This wise husband presented his wife with the registration slip (paid in full) and ten coupons for baby-sitting.

Encouraging your mate is an investment; as your mate develops confidence and competence, you will receive the dividends.

Be a praiser

The word *praise* comes from a Latin word that means "worth," indicating a vital connection between the two. Webster's defines praise as "to commend the worth of; to glorify God; commendation."

Let us add our own definition of praise to the above.

1. *Praise is describing what you appreciate about your mate.* "I like the way you really listen to me." "I appreciate your thoughtfulness in calling me when you're going to be late for dinner."

2. *Praise is affirming what your mate is becoming.* Goethe said: "If you treat a man as he is, he will stay as he is. If you treat him as if he were what he ought to be and could be, he will become that bigger and better man." Begin to look at your mate through Goethe's eyes. Jesus looked at impulsive Peter and called him a rock!

3. *Praise is sincere.* Flattery is not praise. Flattery is insincere and makes the recipient uncomfortable. Flattery is counterfeit praise. Claudia says:

> If Dave told me I was the best cook in the whole world, I could definitely question his sincerity. But if he tells me he appreciates my ability to pull together a meal for unexpected company and remain unhassled, he's believable and I appreciate it! At the same time, I can praise him for losing five pounds and keeping his body in good physical condition, but he would probably not believe me if I told him he was another Charles Atlas.

4. *Praise is verbal.* We can have all kinds of nice thoughts about our mates, but only when they are verbalized is power released. How much praise power have you released today? Perhaps there are no positive thoughts in your head to release. Negative talk is always preceded by negative thoughts.

Philippians 4:8 gives us the solution for this dilemma:

"Finally, brethren, whatever is true . . . honorable . . . right . . . pure . . . lovely . . . of good repute, if there is any excellence and if anything worthy of praise, let your mind dwell on these things." When we begin to apply this verse, we will begin to think in a new pattern, with resulting new verbal habits. Positive thoughts and praise are worth developing. However, habits take time and persistence to develop, so be prepared to persevere!

Recently, a group of wives were studying how to better praise their husbands. Most of the wives sadly admitted that they were not in the habit of praising their mates. They committed to each other and to God to praise their husbands five times during the next week. One friend said at the end of that week, "It felt so strange to hear words of encouragement and praise come out of my lips."

Think about today or yesterday. How many times did you criticize your mate? How many times did you praise your mate? Remember that praise is verbal, and then get with it!

Here are some practical tips for praising one another:

1. Be specific.

   Examples:

   "I appreciate always knowing I'm going to find clean underwear in my dresser each morning."

   "I appreciate your initiative and creativity in our sexual relationship."

2. Describe, don't evaluate.

   Examples:

   Right: "I like the way you kiss me good-bye before I go to work."

   Wrong: "You are the best kisser in the whole world!" (How would you know?)

3. Be sincere; avoid exaggeration.

   Examples of exaggeration:

   "You're the best cook in the whole world!"

   "With your build you should be Mr. America!"

4. Don't overlook written praise:

   a. Notes and jingles.

   b. Thanksgiving or birthday acrostics. Claudia did an acrostic for Dave last Thanksgiving. It looked something like this:

Dave is . . .

T ruthful

H elpful

A thletic

N ice

K ind

S uper

G reat dad

I ntelligent

V ery creative lover

I nteresting

N ever a bore

G od's good gift to me!

Use stick-on letters to dress it up and make your acrostic!

   c. A list of things you appreciate about your mate. One clever husband made a list of thirty-one things he appreciated about his wife. He typed them, cut them up, folded them, put them in capsules, and gave them to his wife with the following prescription: "Take one a day for a month." What a tonic for self-esteem!

   d. Coupons for cashing. Dave relates, "Each Thanksgiving Claudia gives me and the boys an 'I'm thankful for you' coupon book. It's become a real tradition and one that continually reminds us that we are special to her." Some of the things she has included are:

   (1) Free—one back rub with hot oil!

   (2) Breakfast in bed

   (3) Dinner for two at your favorite restaurant (Claudia pays)

5. Give a gift for no reason at all.

This can be small and inexpensive, but the message related is big and priceless.

6. Plan a special person's party.

Dave tells about a party he remembers.

Father's Day, 1980, I'll never forget it! It had been a hectic month—much to do plus a heavy travel schedule which included Father's Day weekend. I arrived home in the late afternoon on Father's Day to be greeted by a surprise party in my honor. Claudia and the boys gave me the nicest Father's Day gift I had ever received. They had spent the whole rainy weekend going through our old slides and had put together a slide show of our family. There were slides from when Claudia and I were dating and a documentary of the birth of each boy, complete with commentary and musical background. Claudia and the boys all participated and at the end gave a tribute to me as a father and husband. Did I feel special? Did I feel appreciated? You bet!

7. Praise often.

On Date 4 you will have the opportunity to begin developing a new habit—the habit of praise. So as you begin this date, remember to (1) concentrate on the strengths, (2) build self-worth, and (3) develop the habit of praise. What changes would take place in the majority of marriages today if we all adopted this strategy!

PROJECT
BUILDING EACH OTHER UP

1. List ways your wife has encouraged you in the past.

   1. *get self in gear*

   2.

   3.

2. List ways you would like your wife to encourage you in the future.

   1.

   2.

   3.

3. In what areas of life do you feel most competent?

4. Is there an area in which you would like to develop competence (Sports, crafts, hobbies, education, etc.)?

5. What can you do to encourage your wife to develop competence in a specific area?

PROJECT
BUILDING EACH OTHER UP

1. List ways your husband has encouraged you in the past.

   1. As a wife + mother
   2. to get a masters degree + administrative credential
   3. to become acquainted/attend CWC etc.
      learn to garden

2. List ways you would like your husband to encourage you in the future.

   1. Learn computer.
   2. lose weight - better health
   3. manage time -

3. In what areas of life do you feel most competent?

   Money management
   Time management

4. Is there an area in which you would like to develop competence (Sports, crafts, hobbies, education, etc.)?

   tennis;
   skiing
   computer.

5. What can you do to encourage your husband to develop competence in a specific area? Real estate business if he want to do that. Money awareness.
   Golf   Lose weight/weight
   Skiing   management

DATE FOUR

DATE NIGHT

Let the wife choose the place to go.

Discuss question 1, letting the wife go first.

Discuss question 2, letting the husband go first.

Each shares answers to 3, 4, and 5. Discuss (if time permits).

Do something just for fun—bowling, tennis, swimming, taking a walk, etc. The only stipulations are that you must *go alone* (together), and you must be *able to communicate* (that rules out movies and TV).

ASSIGNMENT

Try to build up your mate in some area each day. Be gracious and appreciative when he or she builds you up. And avoid saying, "Oh, you had to do that—it's our assignment!"

Read Chapter 5.

EXTRA READING FOR THE EAGER BEAVER

1 Peter 3:8–11

Galloway, Dale. *We're Making Our Home a Happy Place.* Wheaton, Ill.: Tyndale, 1976.

Meredith, Don. *Becoming One.* Nashville: Thomas Nelson, 1979.

DATE FIVE

Purposes: 1. To learn how to better communicate my feelings to my mate.
2. To learn to attack the problem instead of my mate.

Time Commitment: One evening, and one to two hours of preparation.

Preparation:

BOTH: Read Chapter 5: "Communicating Our Feelings." Fill out Project 5, being careful to follow the instructions.

COMMUNICATING OUR FEELINGS

An experiment was conducted to determine the amount of conversation that takes place between the average husband and wife in a normal week. The participants wore portable electronic microphones that measured every word spoken, from "Pass the butter" to "Hi, I'm home. What's for dinner?"

How much time would you guess the average couple spent talking to (or at) each other. An hour a day? No, not seven hours a week, not even one hour, or thirty minutes. Would you believe the average communication time was seventeen minutes *a week*?[1]

What has happened to communication in the average marriage today? Certainly none of us got married and then took a vow of silence. We don't *plan* to stop communicating with each other. What is it that makes people stop communicating with each other. What is it that makes people stop talking to the one person with whom they have chosen to spend the rest of their lives?

No team can survive without communication, so what's a mate to do who wants to unclog those communication lines? May we suggest three things:

1. Desire to communicate.
2. Understand what communication is and try to avoid common mistakes.
3. Learn to communicate on a feelings level.

Communication—I want it!

Communication—only one word, but so vital to any relationship, especially the marital one! The key to good communication begins with the *desire* to communicate.

When we were in Germany several years ago we met Carl. A strong friendship began to develop. One evening we had Carl and his wife, Anna, for dinner. At this point our ability to speak German was below zero. Since Carl's English was passable, we spoke English the whole evening. Anna, who knew not a word of English, was completely left out of the conversation.

A few weeks later (with a few German words in our vocabulary) we were invited to their home for dinner. Remembering our last evening together and how left out Anna had been, we were determined to at least try to communicate with them in German. Hand motions, pantomime, dictionaries, and all sorts of funny gestures enabled us to spend a relatively fun evening together, and our friendship continued to develop. The key was ardently wanting to understand and to communicate with one another.

That sounds simple, but this attitude of wanting to communicate is lacking in many of the conversations in the world today. People often speak to express their own ideas and to justify themselves, not really listening to the other person. Too many conversations become dialogues of the deaf! In business, ignoring good communication can spell disaster and financial failure. In international affairs it can lead to war.

In marriage, poor communication leads to frustration, misunderstandings, alienation, and even divorce. When we talk about communication in marriage we are not talking about an optional exercise; we are talking about its very breath of life. Our son Jarrett commented, "If communication is the breath of life in any marriage, then *Ten Dates for Mates* is the mouthwash!"

What is communication?

Webster's defines communication as, "to impart, to transmit; to give information; to have a meaningful relationship." The third definition is just as important as the first two! We suggest another definition: "Communication exists when another person hears what you said and understands what you meant by what you said." Merely saying the words doesn't mean we've really communicated at all.

The total message

A few years ago Kodak did a study to determine what makes up "the total message" in communication. These are the results.

1. The words actually spoken made up only 7 percent of the total message.

2. Our nonverbal communication accounts for 55 percent of the total message. This includes such things as shrugs, stares, and glares. Picture a wife trying to talk to her husband while his head is buried in the evening paper or his eyes are glued to the TV set. Have you ever said "O.K." when it really wasn't O.K.? Your tone of voice can completely reverse the message. There is no colder place to be than with a couple who are saying the right words, while underneath is bitterness, hostility, and a totally different message.

3. Tone of voice accounts for the other 38 percent of the total message. This includes the sighs and nagging tones that creep into our conversations.[2]

The lost art of listening

We can understand all about nonverbal communication and be tuned in to saying things in the right way, but unless we are good listeners our communication skills will still be deficient. We were surprised to read in Norman Wright's book *Communication: Key to Your Marriage* that it is estimated that most people hear only 20 percent of what is said to them. How do you think you rate in the area of listening? Are you too busy thinking of what you are going to say next to hear what your mate is saying to you? Norman Wright gives the following three suggestions to raise our listening score:

1. One cannot listen intently unless one's mouth is shut!
2. Listening effectively means that when someone is talking, you are not thinking about what you are going to say when the other person stops talking.
3. Listening is more than politely waiting for your turn to speak.[3]

Meet the Arps

Included in our Marriage Alive Seminar in the session on communication are two short skits in which we try to demonstrate *how not to* and *how to* communicate. The first is an imaginary (at least we hope it is!) conversation at the Arps:

CLAUDIA: I believe it's time for my appointment with you.

DAVE: Oh, yes, I noticed you were on my schedule for today. This is a real good idea, scheduling in an hour each month just to talk, but today we'll have to make it quick because I only have thirty minutes. I've just got to finish the seminar on communication for the marriage conference next week.

CLAUDIA: It's great to see I'm such a high priority in your life! If you don't treat me better, one day I may not be here. What would that do to your family image?

DAVE: Now Claudia, don't be so sensitive. It just takes a lot of time to run a family ministry.

CLAUDIA: I want to tell you something for your own good. If you would just organize your time better . . .

DAVE: (interrupts) Speaking of time—we're down to twenty minutes. What was it you wanted to talk about?

CLAUDIA: We need to plan our vacation. I was thinking about it and I have decided we should go to Boston. It would be so educational for the children. I've already written and gotten hotel reservations. They are a little expensive, but if you can afford a new camera with all the attachments, you can certainly take us to Boston!

DAVE: *Hold it!* You're just like your Aunt Gertrude, trying to plan everybody's life for them. I told you last month I didn't want to go to Boston. We are going to the mountains. Period!

CLAUDIA: (looking away and mumbling under her breath) Maybe he'll slip and fall off a cliff! (to Dave) The trouble with you is you never consider the children and you're always late—and leave my aunt out of it. She warned me about you! And what about your mother? Talk about a troublemaker! I remember five years ago when . . .

DAVE: (interrupts again) Oh, why can't a woman think like a man! Why do you always have to be so sensitive and touchy?

CLAUDIA: (starts to cry) Touchy—(sniff)—who, me? I'm not sensitive. It's just that you don't love me and you're mean and inconsiderate!

DAVE: Cut the tears! I think I've got a solution. Why don't you and the kids go to Boston and I'll go to the mountains and get some peace and quiet?

CLAUDIA: That's just fine with me!

DAVE: Oh, time's up. But I need to know if you're going with me to the marriage conference next week.

CLAUDIA: Yes, O.K. I need some time away from the children anyway.

DAVE: Say, I'm really glad we've started taking an hour each month to communicate. It's such a good idea that I'm going to add it to my seminar. Let's set our time for next month.

Make a list of all the communication mistakes we made. Then compare your list with ours.

What we did wrong:
1. Used absolute words like "never" and "always"
2. Interrupted
3. Countercomplained
4. Brought up in-laws and relatives in a negative way
5. Used sarcasm
6. Made threats
7. Brought up the past
8. Shifted topics
9. Used emotional talk, like crying (Once when we came to this point in our seminar, one of the participants commented, "You're not going to take that one away from us, are you? That's my best weapon!")
10. Used "why" questions and "you" statements (When we begin sentences with these two words, they tend to attack, definitely not aiding communication!)

11. Called names
12. Avoided topics

How to start a fight

Ann Landers gives the following four suggestions if you really want to wreck your communication. Start any sentence with one of these four phrases and watch the sparks fly! Avoid their use and you'll be the winner.

1. "The trouble with you is . . ."
2. "I am going to tell you something for your own good . . ."
3. "I've put off mentioning this because I know how sensitive you are . . ."
4. "You aren't going to like what I have to say, but please pay me the courtesy to hear me out . . ."

For the *worst* in communication, attack the person instead of the problem.

Is silence golden?

We've now seen what bad communication can be. What about *no* communication? Consider the couple who have endured another quiet evening of frozen communication. Finally, the wife pulls up a chair and reads her unresponsive husband a communication report of his evening's verbal contributions. It went something like this:

8:00 p.m. "Hi, I'm home."
8:15 p.m. "Stew again? Can't we ever have anything different?"
9:00 p.m. "Where's my new magazine I was reading?"
10:00 p.m. "Anything to eat? I'm still hungry."

"How's that?" she asks. "The total verbal output from you for a whole evening is twenty-four words!"

"Look," he replies, "If you wanted a conversationalist you should have married Johnny Carson!"

"All I want," she says sadly, "is someone to talk to me and to really care. You come home, say 'Hi,' and clam up."

"No," he says, "You've got it all wrong! I come home and I can tell by the way you look that you're upset that I'm late again. I know silence is my only hope—so I withdraw."

"You've got it reversed," says his wife. "You give me the silent treatment and the only way I can get any words out of you is to do a little prodding."

Suddenly it dawns on them that they are both describing the same situation, but each blames the other for starting it! They're in a nag-withdraw-nag-withdraw pattern and holding. Who really cares what came first, the nagging or the withdrawing? The important question is, how do they break the cycle?

Perhaps you've found yourself in a similar situation, spending quiet evenings avoiding topics and feeling the walls of blocked communication. What can we do to tear down those walls? Good news—we've already begun!

On the first date we reemphasized the importance of building our marriage on the right foundational principles—leaving, cleaving, and becoming one. On the second date we shared our expectations in marriage. The third date gave us many new insights into how we are different and how we can fit together as a team. We also learned how to deal with our wrong responses. Last week, on Date 4, we had the opportunity to practice praise and to build up our mates.

All these previous dates are helping us to tear down those walls and be more open with one another. This produces an atmosphere that enables us to communicate on a more intimate level, to share our real feelings, to read the mood, and to get the hidden agenda out on the table. So let's move on to some positive tips for communicating.

Communicating on a feelings level

A relationship is only as deep as its communication level. Unless we can share our real feelings with each other—our hurts, fears, dreams, and inner longings—our communication will remain on a surface level. In a marriage with only surface communication, the husband and wife are little more than roommates, two people living under one roof with no deep relationship or shared hopes and dreams. Why do so many people today settle for shallow communication and hold their feelings tightly inside? Could it be that we are afraid of revealing our inner selves to each other?

When we share our feelings with one another, we disclose what is going on inside and we make ourselves vulnerable. Instead of only discussing the facts (that is, talking about what we are doing and where we are going), we need to be willing to deal with our emotions and feelings in our conversations. However, we may sometimes hesitate to share our feelings, wondering, "How am I going to come out of this encounter feeling good about myself?" Feelings are fragile and we must handle them with care.

We would like to suggest a simple formula for expressing your feelings to your mate. We have used it for a number of years. It is safe, simple, and nonthreatening when used in love and with the right attitude.[4]

The first part of the formula is to state clearly and directly (but in love), *"Let me tell you how I feel*. I feel (happy, joyful, satisfied, hurt, disappointed, angry, frustrated, resentful, anxious, etc.)."

Don't confuse "I feel" with "I think." If you can substitute "I think" for "I feel," then it is not a feeling but a thought. For instance, "I feel that you hurt me!" expresses a thought and judgment, not a feeling. The statement is also directed to the other person and not toward ourselves. It is much safer to direct the statement toward ourselves, like: "I feel hurt." This is a feeling, not a thought or judgment. Feelings can also be stated using the words "I am," as in "I am hurt." Dave gives an example.

Having my office in our home has some advantages, but also several built-in disadvantages, one of which is that my wife and three sons help to keep my desk top in disarray. Boy, is this frustrating to me! They are improving, but from time to time I still have to remind them of my frustration. To apply the Feelings Formula to this situation, I say to my wife and sons, "I am frustrated and angry that my desk is messed up. It is hard to work with all these foreign objects. Could you possibly help me keep it clear of things that don't belong there?"

This is expressing a feeling or emotion. Now if I said, "I feel that you all have been inconsiderate of me by dumping your odds and ends on my desk," I am expressing a judgment or thought, but not a feeling.

We want to express inward feelings and emotions that reflect back to us, and avoid attacking the other person. Remember, a feeling is neither right nor wrong; it just is! And that is what you want to communicate—how you feel.

After you have stated clearly and in love how you feel, ask, *"Now tell me how you feel."* Then be prepared to listen! Don't judge feelings; if you don't understand your mate's feelings you can say something like, "I don't understand why you feel this way, but I accept the fact that you do, and I will try to understand and act in accordance." How can we argue with someone's feelings?

Robert was driving with his dad when they began to discuss Robert's older brother. "Dad, I really feel put down around Ben," he said. His dad responded, "Why, you shouldn't feel that way. There is no basis at all for it." The conversation was ended, and Robert retreated to safer subjects like the weather, soccer, and the latest political crisis.

If Robert's dad had followed the Feelings Formula, the conversation could have continued something like this: "Gee, son, I never realized you felt that way. Tell me more about how you feel. What happens inside you that makes you feel that way?" This approach could have led to an in-depth conversation that might have helped Robert work through his feelings about his brother. At any rate, he would have benefited from having a dad who felt his feelings were valid and was willing to listen to them.

Have you gotten in the habit of surface conversations? Are there areas where you have been hesitant to share your real feelings with your mate? On Date 5 you will have the opportunity to break out of old habit patterns and put the Feelings Formula to work in your marital relationship. We need to express our feelings to our mates, but in a constructive, nondamaging way.

Before you get started, let's take another short visit to the Arps and see if they have picked up any communication tips!

The Arps revisited

Note: A *real* visit to the Arps might reveal less than perfect communication, as it is much easier to write a skit than to live it out in the heat of everyday life!

CLAUDIA: Dave, I'm really glad we've started taking time together each week just to communicate and share our feelings with each other.

DAVE: With such busy schedules, we know how confusing things can get if we don't take time to communicate. Tuesday evenings are really working out well as our date night.

CLAUDIA: Yes, I guess if we're going to do seminars on communication in marriage, this is one area we need to continually work on ourselves!

DAVE: By the way, today I finished revising the rough daft that we did for the talk on communication. We need to set a time to go over it together. I'd really like to know your thoughts and suggestions before having it typed. Could we do that tomorrow morning?

CLAUDIA: Fine. It makes me feel good to be included. How do you feel about my participation in the seminars?

DAVE: It adds to have your perspective, and I appreciate your help. Since we have been pushing to rework the seminar, we haven't taken time to make vacation plans since our last ones fell through last month. I thought we could talk about it tonight and bring the children in on it Friday night during our regular family night. On our family plan, we're scheduled to go to Boston. How do you feel about this?

CLAUDIA: I was disappointed when our original plans fell through, but I wonder if after the seminar is the best time to go. I know that Boston was my idea and not your first choice.

DAVE: That's true, but we had agreed that we wanted the boys to see Boston and that it would be educational for them. But honestly, I do feel frustrated at the thought of driving all the way to Boston after the seminar.

CLAUDIA: Perhaps we can come up with an alternative plan.

DAVE: Claudia, how do you feel about this? I know how much you want to go to Boston and we've delayed this trip two times already.

CLAUDIA: To be honest, I am a little disappointed to have to put it off again, but I know you understand how I feel and that makes all the difference in the world! So, if we can reschedule it for another time, it's O.K. with me.

DAVE: What about in November when the boys have a week free from school? We wouldn't have to fight the summer traffic and we would miss the heat!

CLAUDIA: O.K. It's just so good to know you care. What about a weekend in the mountains after the seminar without the children? We could have the time just to relax and enjoy each other.

DAVE: Sold!

CLAUDIA: Dave, I have a problem, and I'd like to tell you about it. I feel very frustrated when we are late. I'm a time-oriented person, and it really bugs me when I am late. For me it is important to be on time. Could we work at getting to church on time this Sunday?

DAVE: That is frustrating for you, isn't it, when we are late? I'm not as time-oriented as you are. What can I do to help us get there on time?"

CLAUDIA: If we got up a little earlier that would really help.

DAVE: I could organize the boys while you fix breakfast. Together we'll work on it.

Stop and list the things we did right, remembering that we are never quite that perfect! Compare your list with ours.

What we did right:

1. We scheduled time for communicating with each other each week away from home, children, dogs, and phone.
2. We each demonstrated a willingness to continue working at communication. None of us will ever arrive or reach perfection in this area.
3. We used the Feelings Formula and expressed our real thoughts and feelings.
4. We did not judge feelings.
5. We expressed appreciation and built each other up.
6. You couldn't see it, but we had great eye contact!
7. We used "I" statements and attacked problems, not each other.

For the best in communication, talk on a feelings level and attack the problem—not the person!

Now you are ready to go on to Project 5.[5] Fill out the questionnaire before your date, and be prepared for a good time of communicating with your mate.

1. Alan Loy McGinniss, *The Friendship Factor: How to Get Closer to the People You Care For* (Minneapolis: Augsburg Publishing House, 1979), pp. 103, 104.

2. H. Norman Wright, *Communication and Conflict Resolution in Marriage* (Elgin, Ill.: David C. Cook, 1977), p. 6.

3. H. Norman Wright, *Communication: Key to Your Marriage* (Glendale, Calif.: Regal, 1974), p. 55.

4. William G. Clarke, *Marriage* (6505 N. Himes Ave., Tampa, Fla. 33614: Marriage and Family Enrichment Institutes, 1974), p. P13.

5. Ibid., adapted from pp. G8–G16.

PROJECT
COMMUNICATING OUR FEELINGS

INSTRUCTIONS

1. Fill out questionnaire before date night.
2. Be honest, yet never unkind. After serious thought, write what you feel. This can be valuable information for both you and your wife.
3. Write your lists independently of each other. Do not compare or discuss them with each other until your date night.
4. Be specific and positive.

    Examples: "I like it when the house is neat when I get home." "I love it when she shows interest and enthusiasm for sexual relations." "I like it when she deliberately takes time to be with me."

QUESTIONNAIRE

1. List three things your wife does that please you. Be specific. You can include little things or big things.

Example: DAVE: "I like it when Claudia protects me from interruptions."

    1.

    2.

    3.

2. List three things you would like your wife to do more often. Be positive and specific.

Example: DAVE: "Take me out for a cup of coffee or a scoop of ice cream when she wants to talk."

    1.

    2.

    3.

3. List three things you think your wife would like you to do more often. Be positive and specific.

Example: DAVE: "Take her to the opera!"

    1.

    2.

    3.

4. In what ways would you like your wife to let you know you are appreciated?

Example: DAVE: "I like receiving your special little notes."

    1.

    2.

    3.

5. Are you somewhat inhibited in communicating with your wife honestly and openly and in sharing your feelings as well as your thoughts?

_____Yes   _____No   _____Sometimes

If "yes" or "sometimes," why do you think this is so?

6. Are you open to learning some new ways of communicating (for example, using the Feelings Formula)?

_____ Yes   _____ No

7. List two or more of your happiest memories in your relationship over the years.

Example: DAVE: "That special time in Adelboden!"

1.

2.

8. Do you often have positive thoughts about your mate?

_____ Yes   _____ No

If yes, do you express these thoughts to her?

_____ Often   _____ Sometimes   _____ Seldom

9. List three times in your marriage when you have felt really close to your wife (not in order of priority).

Example: DAVE: "The weekend I kidnapped you and took you to the mountains."

1.

2.

3.

Why? What made it special?

Example: DAVE: "I really surprised you, and we had time for each other."

1.

2.

3.

10. When you are in need of support, what do you like your wife to do?

Example: DAVE: "Take the initiative in arranging time alone together."

11. What are some of the milestones of your marriage? (A milestone would be a

special event that significantly affected the direction of your lives together.) Explain why it was a milestone.

Example: "For us, one milestone was our move to Germany several years ago. Our marriage today is different because we were forced to deal with cracks in our marriage that probably would have gone undetected and unresolved had we remained in our former situation."

Perhaps a milestone in your marriage will be these ten dates with your mate!

1.

2.

3.

PROJECT
COMMUNICATING OUR FEELINGS

INSTRUCTIONS

1. Fill out questionnaire before date night.
2. Be honest, yet never unkind. After serious thought, write what you feel. This can be valuable information for both you and your husband.
3. Write your lists independently of each other. Do not compare or discuss them with each other until your date night.
4. Be specific and positive.

   Examples: "I like it when he deliberately takes time to be with me." "I like it when he calls to let me know he will be late for dinner."

QUESTIONNAIRE

1. List three things your husband does that please you. Be specific. You can include little things or big things.

Example: CLAUDIA: "I really like the cards you buy me from time to time."

    1.

    2.

    3.

2. List three things you would like your husband to do more often. Be positive and specific.

Example: CLAUDIA: "Surprise me with two tickets to a concert or opera, and then go with me!"

    1.

    2.

    3.

3. List three things you think your husband would like you to do more often. Be positive and specific.

Example: CLAUDIA: "Setting a romantic atmosphere—candles, soft music, etc."

    1.

    2.

    3.

4. In what ways would you like your husband to let you know you are appreciated?

Example: CLAUDIA: "I love to get flowers."

    1.

    2.

    3.

5. Are you somewhat inhibited in communicating with your husband honestly and openly and in sharing your feelings as well as your thoughts?

_____Yes   _____No   _____Sometimes

If "yes" or "sometimes," why do you think this is so?

6. Are you open to learning some new ways of communicating (for example, using the Feelings Formula)?

_____Yes   _____No

7. List two or more of your happiest memories in your relationship over the years.

Example: CLAUDIA: "That special picnic for two at the lake!"

    1.

    2.

8. Do you often have positive thoughts about your husband?

_____Yes   _____No

If yes, do you express these thoughts to him?

_____Often   _____Sometimes   _____Seldom

9. List three times in your marriage when you have felt really close to your husband (not in order of priority).

Example: CLAUDIA: "When we took a working vacation to Zurich and wrote out our *Marriage Alive* Seminar for the first time."

    1.

    2.

    3.

Why? What made it special?

Example: CLAUDIA: "We were alone together, committed to the same purpose, and had time to work, play, and relax."

    1.

    2.

    3.

10. When you are in need of support, what do you like your husband to do?

Example: CLAUDIA: "Take the initiative in arranging time alone together."

11. What are some of the milestones of your marriage? (A milestone would be a

special event that significantly affected the direction of your lives together.) Explain why it was a milestone.

Example: "For us, one milestone was our move to Germany several years ago. Our marriage today is different because we were forced to deal with cracks in our marriage that probably would have gone undetected and unresolved had we remained in our former situation."

Perhaps a milestone in your marriage will be these ten dates with your mate!

1.

2.

3.

DATE FIVE

DATE NIGHT

Choose a location that will allow you to talk quietly—perhaps a picnic in a park. Go through the communication questionnaire, using these guidelines:

1. Exchange lists.

2. Discuss item by item, expressing your feelings when you agree and when you disagree. Alternate going first.

3. Be prepared for some surprises and for a lot of helpful information. The insights gained during this exercise can open new opportunities for growth and intimacy in your marriage.

ASSIGNMENT

Choose together one or two communication tips and agree to use them for the next week, like:

1. Avoid "you" statements.
2. No "why" questions.
3. Use the Feelings Formula.

Read Chapter 6.

EXTRA READING FOR THE EAGER BEAVER

Augsburger, David. *Caring Enough to Confront.* (rev. ed.) Glendale, Calif.: Regal, 1980.

Clarke, William G. *Marriage.* 6505 N. Himes Ave., Tampa, Fla. 33614: Marriage and Family Enrichment Institutes, 1974.

Wright, Norman. *Communication: Key to Your Marriage.* Glendale, Cal.: Regal, 1974.

DATE SIX

Purpose: To better understand our God-given roles as husband and wife.

Time Commitment: One evening, and one hour of preparation.

Preparation:

BOTH: Read Chapter 6: "Realizing Our Roles." Go through checklist, filling out your own and then how you think your spouse will rate himself or herself.

REALIZING OUR ROLES

THE CONNECTION

Long, long ago, as you may know,
It was most often said
That in all homes which were well run
The husband was the head.

Since ancient times there have been rhymes
And views about which spouse
Would occupy the place of head
In any well run house.

It seemed to me that there could be
Full freedom from this strife
If one's position was made clear
Concerning man and wife.

So wife and I thought we would try
To save our home from wreck.
She said, "Of course, you be the head;
I'll only be the neck."

And now I see the loyalty
And wisdom of her plan,
And confidently recommend
The same to every man.

But I request you make this test;
Learn what you may expect;
Just try to move your head without
Permission from your neck![1]

Joel Stembridge

This couple had worked our their roles, but they were confused about their positions. Too many times the husband and wife are neck and neck in a race to see who is going to be the head!

Many misconceptions

Today there are many different views and misconceptions of marriage. Let's consider the husband's role in marriage today. Some picture him as a bureaucratic ruler who never makes a mistake (or at least won't admit that he has) and continually reminds those around him, "I'm the boss in my house. When I tell my wife to jump, she not only jumps but she asks, 'How far?'" On the other extreme is pictured the husband who is simply a pawn, weak and spineless, whose wife leads him by the nose and directs his life. Both views are warped!

And what about the wife? Is she to be a "Yes, dear," "Whatever you say, dear," mate—there to serve with no interest and personality of her own? Of course not! But the other extreme is just as ridiculous. Picture the wife who is not much more than a roommate, pursuing her own things, whether it's to climb the corporate ladder or to beat Chris Evert-Lloyd in tennis. Whatever her interests are, she is more concerned about developing her own individuality than in being a wife, and anything that hinders her—including her man—watch out!

It may sound strange, but it's true: Since being married, the Carvers have lived in different states. The wife pursues an acting career and lives in California. The husband, a professor, lives in a university town in the east. The only time they manage to get together is for holidays.

In this day of individuality you can find almost any kind of marriage; however, most of these self-designed arrangements just don't work. Where can we go to find a workable arrangement? In Chapter 1 we said that in order to come to the right solution or conclusion we must start with the right premise. So back we go to the first marriage manual. God's order for husbands and wives works because He's the One who created marriage in the first place! Let's consider the following instructions.

Back to the marriage manual

Ephesians 5:21–33:

Be subject to one another in the fear of Christ. Wives, be subject to your own husbands, as to the Lord. For the husband is the head of the wife, as Christ also is the head of the church, He Himself being the Savior of the body. But as the church is subject to Christ, so also the wives ought to be to their husbands in everything. Husbands, love your wives, just as Christ also loved the church and gave Himself up for her; that He might sanctify her, having cleansed her by the washing of water with the word, that He might present to Himself the church in all her glory, having no spot or wrinkle or any such thing; but that she should be holy and blameless. So husbands ought also to love their own wives as their own bodies. He who loves his own wife loves himself; for no one ever hated his own flesh, but nourishes and cherishes it, just as Christ also does the church, because we are members of His body. For this cause a man shall leave his father and mother, and shall cleave to his wife; and the two shall become one flesh. This mystery is great; but I am speaking with reference to Christ and the church. Nevertheless, let each individual among you also love his own wife even as himself; and let the wife see to it that she respect her husband.

Three principles from these verses will help us find our right roles.
1. The husband is to lead and love.
2. The wife is to follow and encourage.
3. Both are to mutually respect each other.

Husband: Leader and lover

Any organization or group needs a head, or sheer anarchy will result. A head is also needed in marriage, and God has delegated this role to the husband. But he is not to be a bureaucratic leader; instead, he is to demonstrate the same attitude Christ demonstrated. Jesus was willing to give up His life for the church. Husband, are you willing to make that kind of sacrifice for your wife? As you give her leadership, do you exhibit the same depth of love for her that you have for yourself? We note that in the Ephesians passage we find once again the three important principles from Chapter

1—to leave, to cleave, and to be one. These three principles are enhanced when they are lived out within a framework of God's order for husbands and wives.

Job description: Headship with love

As a husband relates to his wife, he is to demonstrate the following characteristics. (Husbands, check yourselves and see how you are doing!)

1. He is to be unselfish.
2. He is to be humble.
3. He is to be willing to put his wife first and be self-sacrificing.
4. He is to be understanding and sensitive to her and to her needs.

As he incorporates these qualities into his marriage relationship, he can then fulfill his job: to give leadership with love. There is no place in God's order for a husband who is a bully or a pawn.

How does this work out in the nitty-gritty of married life?

Husband, let's say you've come home from a busy day at the office. You're tired of work and tired of people. All you really want to do is to crawl into your easy chair and read the paper in total silence and peace. *But* you are met at the door by your wife who, having been with the small children all day long, is eager to have some adult conversation for a change. What do you do? Are you willing to empathize with your wife and sacrifice or delay for a few minutes your own desires in order to meet a need in her life? Are you willing to follow her into the kitchen, take a seat for a few minutes, and listen to her tell you all about the baby's new tooth, who she saw at the grocery store, or whatever she wants to talk about. Then you qualify as an A-1 leader and lover.

On the other hand, wives can be A-1 helpers. One husband we know has an extremely high-pressure job. One or two nights a month he comes home emotionally drained, and says, "Honey, give me just thirty minutes to myself alone in our room and I'll be fine." Rather than insisting she unload her woes of the day, she makes sure their six kids honor Dad's request for quiet. Then, after a half hour or so, Dad is ready to join the family fun for the evening.

Let's take another situation. There is a major decision to be made, but even after much discussion you and your wife disagree. You understand her position clearly, but you feel you are right. What do you do? God says it's your responsibility to make that final decision, and it's you He will hold responsible for the final outcome. Headship can be heavy; sometimes it seems wives have the easiest part!

Wife: Helpmate and encourager

A helpmate and encourager isn't to be a maid and a "yes sir" woman, but neither is she to be such an individualist that she only considers her life and ambitions. In the Ephesians passage we see she is to be a helper who is *suited* for her mate. She is to be his completer and is to stand alongside him and be his encourager.

Look behind the great men of today and you will find women who are supporting them and encouraging them on to greatness. Every wife has the potential to help her husband be a success or a failure in life! Wives, which do you choose? Follow God's guidelines for relating as a wife and not only will your husband be successful, but you will, too.

A wife is to demonstrate the following characteristics:
1. She is willing to follow her husband.
2. She has a submissive attitude.
3. She has a gentle and quiet spirit.
4. She is committed, dedicated, and loving.[2]

Submission: A red-flag word

In today's world the word *submission* causes campaigners for the liberation of women to stand up and spit nails in anger. We believe that true liberation for married women comes from fitting in with God's plan and His order for marriage. Submission in marriage is the wife's willingness to support her home team and let her husband be captain. They are equally valuable players; the husband is not more valuable nor more important, but functionally he is captain of the team. The wife is to be committed to him, to cooperate with him, to support him, and to encourage him, realizing that unless they work together they will both lose the game!

This last decade clearly has shown us that there are two solutions to the husband-wife role dilemma that absolutely do not work: feminism and male chauvinism. How depressing to be male-ist or feminist! It's the old me-first business again, redefined along the lines of gender. The solution isn't me first or us first, but God first. In marriages where Jesus Christ is Lord—where He's first—the husband and wife roles then revolve around Him, and the marriage clicks. We can even get the authority-submission principles down pat, but unless Christ gives life to that relationship it reverts to a shallow legalism. God must be in charge.

Submission is not always easy

It is easy for a wife to follow her husband when she agrees with him, but this is not always the case. Read Claudia's experience.

I tend to be very opinionated and also very verbal. It's hard to willingly follow when you think your husband is dead wrong! But in the end it is an act of the will and not an emotional "wanting to."

In 1973, when we were asked to move to Germany, I was very opposed to the idea. I loved Knoxville, our home, and our friends, and was finding life there quite fulfilling. The last thing I wanted to do was pull up stakes with three boys (ages six and under) and move halfway around the world to a country where I couldn't even understand the language. That was bad enough, but we also were asked to be there in six weeks!

You better believe I didn't remain silent. But after many long discussions and after my pointing out every possible objection, Dave made the decision: "We're moving!" At that point I had to make a decision. Was I willing to submit and follow his leadership? Believe me, it wasn't easy, and the first year there was, from my perspective, a disaster! But now as I look back over the years, I can see God's hand in our lives and the positive results of that move. You will probably never be asked to move to a new continent as I was, but the real issue is whether or not you are willing to follow your husband's leadership in whatever area it is.

Respect is mutual

A loving leader and a faithful follower should live in an atmosphere of mutual respect. Remember that the first verse in the Ephesians passage states: "Be subject to one another."

We as Christians are to have the attitude of being submitted to one another. This implies an underlying foundation of mutual respect. Philippians 2:3 says it this way:

"Do nothing from selfishness or empty conceit, but with humility of mind let each of you regard one another as more important than himself." This simply means we are to think of the other first and be willing to put our mate's needs and desires before our own.

There is no place in marriage for competition. Competing is the opposite of submitting. Someone described mutually submitting as mutually yielding to one another. Suppose the husband wants to go to a ball game and the wife to the opera. Just because the husband is the leader doesn't mean the opera is out and the ball game is in—not if they are following the directive in Philippians 2.

Symptoms of mutual respect

When marriage partners mutually respect each other, it is easy to see that they are on the same team. You don't hear them putting each other down. They have a foundation of mutual respect and they are courteous and kind to one another. Their home has an atmosphere of love and acceptance—no battleground there! They play their positions well, and it's obvious they are winning. How are you doing? Are you playing the right positions? Husband, are you leading your wife in love? Wife, are you voluntarily following and encouraging your husband? Then you are well on the way to being a winning team!

1. Joel Stembridge, *The Other Sheep* (Knoxville, Tenn., 1982), p. 6.

2. Gene Getz, *The Measure of a Family* (Glendale, Calif.: Regal, G/L Publication, 1976), pp. 184, 185.

3. Ibid., pp. 140, 141. Adapted and used by permission.

4. Ibid.

PROJECT
REALIZING OUR ROLES

Go through the following two checklists,[3] checking yourself on the first and then how you think your wife would rate herself on the second. On your date, compare lists and note areas of potential conflict or disagreement. You will be dealing with these on Date 7.

A Husband's Checklist

The following statements are designed to help you evaluate your attitudes and actions toward your wife.

(O)–Often
(S)–Sometimes
(R)–Rarely
(N)–Never

_____ I'm willing to give up something I want to do in order to do something my wife wants to do.

_____ I provide sufficient income for her to meet household and personal expenses.

_____ I trust her to do a good job in the home.

_____ I plan my schedule so I can spend time with her.

_____ I am courteous and always treat her like a lady.

_____ I keep myself physically attractive.

_____ I do what I can to let her know she is frequently in my thoughts.

_____ I listen to her complaints without being threatened.

_____ I communicate regularly what I'm doing, where I'm going, and what my daily schedule involves.

_____ I am on time for meals, and if there are emergencies I call ahead of time.

_____ I become involved with the children.

_____ I help my wife around the house.

_____ I find opportunities for her to get away from the home and the routine—alone or with her friends.

_____ I carve out time for just the two of us to be alone.

_____ I show jealousy toward her friends.

_____ I shout at her, abuse her, or make unreasonable demands upon her.

_____ I provide spiritual leadership for my wife and family.

_____ I allow other things to interfere with my relationship with my wife and family.

List briefly potential areas of conflict or disagreement.

1.

2.

3.

4.

5.

A Wife's Checklist

The following statements are designed to help your wife evaluate her attitudes and actions. How do you think she would rate herself?

(O)–Often (A)*Always*

(S)–Sometimes

(R)–Rarely

(N)–Never

_____ I find it difficult to follow my husband's leadership.

_____ I show jealousy toward his friends or his job.

_____ I complain about his schedule.

_____ I reveal lack of trust.

_____ I usually do what my husband asks me to.

_____ I embarrass him in public.

_____ I respond to him with bitterness in my voice.

_____ I shout or scream at him.

_____ I argue with him.

_____ I allow my friends or activities to interfere with the time I need to meet his needs.

_____ I nag my husband.

_____ I keep our house clean and neat.

_____ I try to make our home a comfortable place for him to live.

_____ I'm available to meet his sexual needs.

_____ I put him down publicly or privately.

_____ I keep myself attractive physically.

_____ I spend money carelessly or foolishly.

_____ I allow others to interfere with my relationship with my husband and family.

List briefly potential areas of conflict or disagreement.

1.

2.

3.

4.

5.

PROJECT
REALIZING OUR ROLES

Go through the following two checklists,[4] checking yourself on the first and then how you think your husband would rate himself on the second. On your date, compare lists and note areas of potential conflict or disagreement. You will be dealing with these on Date 7.

A Wife's Checklist

The following statements are designed to help you evaluate your attitudes and actions toward your husband.

(O)—Often
(S)—Sometimes
(R)—Rarely
(N)—Never

_____ I find it difficult to follow my husband's leadership.

_____ I show jealousy toward his friends or his job.

_____ I complain about his schedule.

_____ I reveal lack of trust.

_____ I usually do what my husband asks me to.

_____ I embarrass him in public.

_____ I respond to him with bitterness in my voice.

_____ I shout or scream at him.

_____ I argue with him.

_____ I allow my friends or activities to interfere with the time I need to meet his needs.

_____ I nag my husband.

_____ I keep our house clean and neat.

_____ I try to make our home a comfortable place for him to live.

_____ I'm available to meet his sexual needs.

_____ I put him down publicly or privately.

_____ I keep myself attractive physically.

_____ I spend money carelessly or foolishly.

_____ I allow others to interfere with my relationship with my husband and family.

List briefly potential areas of conflict or disagreement.

1.

2.

3.

4.

5.

A Husband's Checklist

The following statements are designed to help your husband evaluate his attitudes and actions. How do you think he would rate himself?

(O)–Often
(S)–Sometimes
(R)–Rarely
(N)–Never

_____ I'm willing to give up something I want to do in order to do something my wife wants to do.

_____ I provide sufficient income for her to meet household and personal expenses.

_____ I trust her to do a good job in the home.

_____ I plan my schedule so I can spend time with her.

_____ I am courteous and always treat her like a lady.

_____ I keep myself physically attractive.

_____ I do what I can to let her know she is frequently in my thoughts.

_____ I listen to her complaints without being threatened.

_____ I communicate regularly what I'm doing, where I'm going, and what my daily schedule involves.

_____ I am on time for meals, and if there are emergencies I call ahead of time.

_____ I become involved with the children.

_____ I help my wife around the house.

_____ I find opportunities for her to get away from the home and the routine—alone or with her friends.

_____ I carve out time for just the two of us to be alone.

_____ I show jealousy toward her friends.

_____ I shout at her, abuse her, or make unreasonable demands upon her.

_____ I provide spiritual leadership for my wife and family.

_____ I allow other things to interfere with my relationships with my wife and family.

List briefly potential areas of conflict or disagreement.

1.

2.

3.

4.

5.

DATE SIX

DATE NIGHT

Go to a favorite restaurant for dinner, or go out for coffee and dessert.

Share checklist with each other.

List areas of potential conflict or disagreement. (You will be dealing with these on the next date!)

ASSIGNMENT

Read Chapter 7.

EXTRA READING FOR THE EAGER BEAVER

Dahl, Gerald. *Why Christian Marriages Are Breaking Up.* Nashville: Thomas Nelson, 1979.

Getz, Gene. *The Measure of a Family.* Glendale, Calif.: Regal, 1976.

Hancock, Maxine. *Love, Honor, and Be Free.* Chicago: Moody, 1976.

DATE SEVEN

Purposes: 1. To learn better ways of handling conflict.
2. To resolve one issue.

Time Commitment: One evening, and one hour of preparation.

Preparation:

BOTH: Read Chapter 7: "Resolving Honest Conflict." Fill out Part 1 of Project 7, referring to checklist from Date Six.

RESOLVING HONEST CONFLICT

Most people were shocked when Bill and Barb separated. On the surface they looked like the ideal all-American family with three lovely children, complete with dogs, hamsters, and goldfish. Bill was a businessman with financial success, a position of importance in the community, and a secure future (or so it seemed) until one day Bill left his wife, his family, his job, and his secure future and flew off to Europe with another woman.

But consider another couple—Marg and Ralph. Conflict was present in their relationship from the beginning. They came from totally different backgrounds. Each had a strong personality and they seldom agreed on anything, whether it was child discipline or interior decorating. Yet over the years they have hung together and have achieved a reasonable amount of stability and happiness in their marriage. What makes the difference? Why did one marriage make it and the other crash?

Couple one

Barb was quiet and reserved, but Bill made up for her shyness with his outgoing personality. Their home was filled continually with people. As we first met Bill and Barb we wondered when they ever had any time alone together; the truth was they had very little. Certainly their lives were busy, but was the activity a means of avoiding one another as well as the conflict in their marriage?

In the first years of their marriage when they had differences of opinion (which happened often), Barb would usually yield to Bill's wishes, not even expressing her own feelings. Tension grew in their relationship. Sometimes these tensions developed into heated debates or arguments, but instead of resolving them and clearing the air, Bill and Barb became divided and began to lead separate lives.

It was about this time that Barb took a job outside the home. In this way she could avoid much of the home tension and also provide some financial security for herself and the children. Since she and Bill had grown apart and weren't really able to communicate, she had difficulty trusting him to provide for her financially.

Their quarrels, although still private, were developing into fights. Both were beginning to have feelings of rejection. As the children grew older, Bill and Barb became more openly hostile to one another, and open war resulted. One day Bill decided that the best thing for all concerned was for him to leave, and physical separation resulted; emotional separation had already occurred years ago.

Unresolved conflict does not go away. It may be covered over for a while, but eventually it pokes up its ugly head. Consider the following chart.[1]

UNRESOLVED CONFLICT

DIFFERENCE OF OPINION ⟶	"SPAT" ⟶	CONFRONTATION
HEATED DEBATE OR ARGUMENT ⟶	"QUARREL" ⟶	DIVISION
INTENSE PHYSICAL ANGER ⟶	"FIGHT" ⟶	REJECTION
HOSTILITY CONFIRMED ⟶	"WAR" ⟶	SEPARATION

Unresolved conflict grows and grows, progressing through the steps of the above chart until the end result is reached and separation occurs.

Couple two

You will remember that Marg and Ralph also did not get along well from the beginning. They were both very opinionated and very verbal, which sometimes led to very heated discussions. But *both were committed to resolving issues in their marriage when they came up.* At times a third party was needed to help them work through their problems. Often compromise was part of the solution.

They gradually learned how to express their strong feelings without attacking the other person. Time alone was vital in their marriage relationship, and they often tried to go away overnight without the children. Ralph liked surprises, so at times Marg planned a weekend away and told Ralph at the last minute what was in store. Sometimes Ralph would take the initiative and write in his calendar—"time with Marg."

When problems arose, they were committed to working them through. Does this mean they have a conflict-free marriage today? *No!* And at times they both still blow it. The difference is they are willing to do whatever it takes to resolve conflict. It is not always easy or convenient, and it can be tiring and discouraging, but Marg and Ralph have discovered that for the success of their marriage, it is vital to work at resolving conflict.

Do you have conflict?

Do you have conflict in your marriage? If you're honest, the answer will be yes. It's an impossibility for two people from two separate backgrounds (complete with differing goals, viewpoints, and points of reference) to agree on everything. Even our three boys, who have the same background and family, do not agree on everything. (Sometimes it seems to us they agree on very little!)

So the question is not, "Do we have conflict in our marriage?"—we all do! Conflict in itself is neither good nor bad, right nor wrong. Conflict simply is! It is how we respond to conflict that is important.

The question then is, "How can we respond in the right way; how can we resolve conflict?" Certainly we are not advocating unreserved expression of all our feelings. This leads to open warfare and many verbal battles in which there are no winners and two casualties! On the other hand, when we ignore conflict the results can be resentment, bitterness, and suppressed anger.

Our goal must be to resolve conflict *and* maintain the relationship. If we are willing to work through our wrong responses and attitudes, our relationship can be strengthened and built in the midst of our differences. Let us consider the following:

1. Potential areas of conflict—what types of things do we argue about?
2. Possible ways to handle conflict—good and bad.
3. Steps for resolving conflict.

POTENTIAL AREAS OF CONFLICT

During your sixth date night you were encouraged to begin a list of potential areas of conflict in your own marital relationship. If you were unable to come up with anything, consider the following areas.

Money

Someone put it this way: "Till debt us do part." Our goal in this chapter is not to give you the solution to money problems, but to help you analyze if this is an area in which you need to work.

Children

Many times the birth of the first child brings conflict—along with dirty diapers and lost sleep! Claudia remembers:

> We had been married for four years when Jarrett was born, and were we ever proud and happy to have our little boy! However, I was not so thrilled at four in the morning when Jarrett was crying and hungry—or worse still, when he was crying and he wasn't hungry or sleepy! The next morning I would find it hard to be my normal cheery self, and as a result I was impatient and short with Dave.
>
> Also, after four years of planning my own schedule during the day, it was a real adjustment to have the continual companionship of our little bundle of joy. Sometimes all I could see was the pile of diapers that needed washing and folding. (That was back in pre-Pampers days!) And where was Dave during all of this? He was at the office enjoying himself.

We consider each of our boys a wonderful gift from God, and they have really brought us much happiness. But the first few months of adjustment can be trying and can make mates vulnerable to conflict with each other.

As the children grow up there are all kinds of opportunities for conflict, considering all the differing philosophies of child rearing. We have found that with teens the list is endless—music, dating, hairstyles, and curfews, to name a few.

Sex

Many people use sex as a weapon, a reward, or a favor. It is probably the area of conflict in marriage that is least openly discussed. The result is often a cold war—and a very cold marital bed! If sex is on your conflict list, don't despair; help is coming in Chapter 8.

In-laws

Often in-laws can become out-laws when mates verbally attack each other's parents. Conflict tends to develop in this area when we ignore the first principle covered in Chapter 1—the commitment to leave, be it our parents or any other relationship that is more important to us than our mate. If this is an area of conflict in your marriage, review Chapter 1 and together agree to work at resolving this issue in your marriage.

Priorities and time management

What are your priorities? Does the way you manage your time reflect them? Do you both agree on your common priorities and time management? If not, expect conflict! Dave relates:

Conflict tends to appear at our home when our priorities get out of order. Because Claudia is an activist, she can get so overcommitted that sometimes there is not enough of her left over for our own family.

Or I can get so involved in a project that I forget my priorities—like the night recently that I went back to the office to use the computer. I was trying to get out some important letters and was so involved in the whole process that I forgot the time. At three-thirty in the morning the phone rang. It was Claudia just getting ready to send out a search party and order flowers for my funeral. My poor time management had opened the door to conflict at the Arps.

What about the husband who has to work twelve-hour days to survive in his job, while his wife is at home with three small children? Unless there is good communication and a real commitment to each other, this can spell conflict.

Little flies in the soup

Consider the little daily things that can irritate:

1. One likes the house as warm as the tropics—the other would make a good Eskimo!

2. One's middle name is *punctuality*—the other's is *late arriver*.

3. One likes that homey lived-in look—the other arranges the magazines on the table at a forty-five-degree angle.

4. One wakes up and gets going with the roosters in the morning—the other begins to enjoy life at midnight.

5. One is a precision toothpaste roller—the other a creative squeezer.

HOW DO YOU HANDLE CONFLICT

Since conflict is a normal part of our lives, how can we deal with it? Sometimes we respond as one or more of our animal friends.[2]

Mr. Turtle—The Withdrawer

When faced with conflict, Mr. Turtle withdraws. He has developed a hard shell of emotional insulation. He just doesn't want to get involved!

Tom was a turtle. Whenever Sally wanted to talk about their future security (a subject Tom would just as soon not discuss) he would withdraw. He wanted to ignore the subject and hope it would go away. He wanted to bury his feelings of insecurity and just not admit that he had failed to plan for their future. Withdrawing into his shell of silence thus became his way of dealing with the conflict in his marriage.

Are you a withdrawer like our turtle friend? Do you withdraw physically, like getting up and walking out of the house? Or maybe your style of withdrawing is to emotionally turn the other person off. Perhaps you withdraw because you feel you can't win anyway. Keep in mind that withdrawing turns off the relationship as well as a possible solution.

Mr. Skunk—The Fighter

Mr. Skunk says, "I'll make you stink first!" He loves to use sarcasm and to accuse: "You did this, and you did that . . ." He'd rather not take responsibility for what *he* did wrong; as a matter of fact, he refuses to!

Tom the turtle's wife, Sally, was a skunk. She responded to Tom's seeming indifference about their future security by trying to make him stink. She would tell him what a mean guy he was, so uncaring and irresponsible in ignoring wise planning for their future. She used statements like, "You just don't care about our children's future education," or "You just think of yourself!" Tom the turtle pulls deeper into his shell while Sally the skunk attacks.

The fighter concentrates on attacking the other person. He would rather make the other person look bad than let his own insecurities show.

Mr. Gorilla—The Winner

Mr. Gorilla is a fighter who always has to win. Two weapons he likes to use are manipulation and intimidation. He has a low self-image, so he wants to look good no matter what the cost! The cost is usually a hurt relationship with the other person. He files away old grudges, hurts, and wrongs to be pulled out and used at the appropriate times.

He is an autocratic ruler, but inside he is timid and afraid. He uses his gruffness to keep others at a distance. A gorilla has a hard time being a good teammate with his mate. He doesn't want to get close enough to reveal his insecurities.

Mr. Chameleon—The Yielder

The chameleon turns colors according to his environment, thus avoiding conflict. He takes on the opinions of those around him. When he is with a quiet group, he is quiet too. When he is with a loud group, he becomes loud. Underneath his changing color, the chameleon is very insecure and afraid to express his real opinion. He desires to always fit in and desperately wants to be accepted. So when he meets conflict, he goes along with the crowd. The yielder will give in to get along with his partner. A habitual yielder often develops a martyr complex and likes to use emotional blackmail.

Mr. Owl—The Avoider

Mr. Owl will do all he can to avoid conflict. He is the intellectualizer; his motto is "Avoid feelings at all cost!" He'll gladly discuss an issue on an intellectual basis, but he has no feelings from his cranium down. He deals with facts, facts, and facts! Mr. Owl usually leaves a trail of hurt feelings. He finds it almost impossible to identify with the other person's feelings because he has few of his own. Since emotions are usually involved in conflict, he avoids conflict like the plague.

Mr. Owl, by the way, has two second cousins. One, Mr. Beaver, avoids conflict by suddenly getting busy. Even the silver gets polished! The other, Mr. Ostrich, avoids conflict by sticking his head in the sand, just ignoring the situation.

What's your style?

Do you identify with any of our animal friends? Perhaps you can identify with more than one of them. At different times we may react to conflict in different ways. But we are not animals; we can choose how we will respond. Sometimes we may yield or withdraw. At other times it may be important to speak up for our position. Often compromise is involved, but our goal in dealing with conflict should be to resolve it. If we habitually respond as our animal friends, we are in trouble.

Resolving conflict involves a willingness to be open with each other and to communicate our real feelings. It involves both partners being willing to yield to each other at times, or to come to a compromise in which each is willing to give a little. It involves committing the time it will take to work through differences to the point where both people are satisfied with the end results. Being willing to work through a conflict builds the relationship without sacrificing individual goals.

Now . . . if the best approach to conflict is to determine to resolve it, how do we go about doing that? We suggest four steps.[3]

STEPS FOR RESOLVING CONFLICT

Step One—Define the problem.

First, we must admit there is a conflict. Write down what it is you are trying to resolve.

Step Two—Identify who has the need for a solution and the other's contribution to the problem.

Write it down.

Step Three—Suggest alternate solutions.

Make a list.

Step Four—Select a plan of action.

The above is a simple problem-solving method, but it can be of great benefit in resolving conflict in marriage. It helps you focus on the problem you are trying to resolve, not on each other.

Let's look at an example.

(1) Define the problem: "I don't like towels left on the bathroom floor!"

(2) Identify who has the need for a solution and the other's contribution to the problem. Wife has the need. Husband leaves wet towels on the floor.

(3) List alternate solutions:

    a. Leave towel on the floor.

    b. Wife picks up towel.

    c. Husband picks up towel.

    d. Use disposable towels and throw away.

    e. Don't use towels and drip dry.

    f. Don't bathe.

    g. Fold towel and put on towel rack.

(4) Plan of action: g.

Let's consider another example:

(1) Define the problem: Husband and wife cannot agree on a bedtime.

(2) Identify who has the need and the other's contribution to the problem. Wife desires husband to go to bed at the same time she does. She is often tired and wants to go to bed early. Husband likes to unwind and watch the late show or read.

(3) List alternate solutions:

    a. Husband forgets the late show and reading and goes to bed whenever his wife wants to.

    b. Wife ignores husband and goes to bed.

    c. Husband says, "I'm the boss and I'll do as I please."

    d. Put TV in bedroom so husband can watch it and wife can go on to sleep.

    e. Wife gets a good book and they read in bed together.

    f. Wife takes a nap in the afternoon so she is more rested and can stay up a little later a night. Husband agrees to go to bed a little earlier.

    g. Husband and wife discuss their week's schedule and decide ahead of time what they would like to see on TV. They talk through their commitments for the week so the wife will know when her husband may need to unwind, and husband will be aware of when his wife may be especially tired. They plan to work at going to bed at the same time as often as possible.

(4) Plan of action: Which would you choose? Go through the list of alternate solutions and identify the different "animal" styles of handling conflict. Now you are ready to fill out Part 1 of Project 7. Fill it out before your date night.

It will be exciting for you to see how—whether turtle, skunk, gorilla, owl, or chameleon—you can learn together to relate and resolve conflict. In this project you will work together at resolving one conflict while building your relationship.

1. James Fairfield, *When You Don't Agree* (Scottdale, Pa.: Herald, 1977), p. 19.

2. We thank Doug Wilson for letting us adapt his illustration of animal characters.

3. H. Norman Wright, *The Pillars of Marriage* (Glendale, Calif.: Regal, 1979), adapted from p. 158.

PROJECT
RESOLVING HONEST CONFLICT

PART 1—Answer the following two questions by yourself, before your date night.

1. Which animal character do you identify with the most in handling conflict? Rank from most often used (1) to least often used (5).

   _____ Mr. Turtle—The Withdrawer

   _____ Mr. Skunk—The Fighter

   _____ Mr. Gorilla—The Winner

   _____ Mr. Chameleon—The Yielder

   _____ Mr. Owl—The Avoider

2. List three or more areas of conflict in your marriage.

   A.

   B.

   C.

   D.

   E.

PART 2—Now, together with your wife, do the following.

Compare your list with your wife's list.

Together, choose *one* mutual area of conflict and go through the four steps of resolving conflict. Remember to use the Feelings Formula as you discuss the area of conflict: "I feel . . ."

   "Now tell me how you feel . . ."

1. Admit there is a conflict—define the problem.
2. Identify who has the need for a solution and the other's contribution to the conflict.

3. Suggest alternate solutions.

   A.

   B.

   C.

   D.
4. Write out a plan of action!

PROJECT
RESOLVING HONEST CONFLICT

PART 1—Answer the following two questions by yourself, before your date night.

1. Which animal character do you identify with the most in handling conflict? Rank from most often used (1) to least often used (5).

_____ Mr. Turtle—The Withdrawer

_____ Mr. Skunk—The Fighter

_____ Mr. Gorilla—The Winner

_____ Mr. Chameleon—The Yielder

_____ Mr. Owl—The Avoider

2. List three or more areas of conflict in your marriage.

A.

B.

C.

D.

E.

PART 2—Now, together with your husband, do the following.

Compare your list with your husband's list.
Together, choose *one* mutual area of conflict and go through the four steps of resolving conflict. Remember to use the Feelings Formula as you discuss the area of conflict: "I feel . . ."

"Now tell me how you feel . . ."

1. Admit there is a conflict—define the problem.
2. Identify who has the need for a solution and the other's contribution to the conflict.

3. Suggest alternate solutions.

    A.

    B.

    C.

    D.
4. Write out a plan of action!

DATE SEVEN

DATE NIGHT

Go to a quiet restaurant or a friend's empty apartment.

Compare lists and do Part 2 of the project, choosing one conflict and going through the four steps of resolving it.

ASSIGNMENT: Read Chapter 8.

EXTRA READING FOR THE EAGER BEAVER

Augsburger, David. *Caring Enough to Confront,* rev. ed. Glendale, Calif.: Regal, 1980.

Fairfield, James. *When You Don't Agree.* Scottdale, Pa.: Herald, 1977.

Wright, Norman. *The Pillars of Marriage.* Glendale, Calif.: Regal, 1979.

DATE EIGHT

Purposes: 1. To become more creative in our love life.
2. To verbally communicate more openly in this area!

Time Commitment: We recommend an overnight getaway. If this is absolutely impossible, then set aside four to six hours during an evening.

Preparation:

BOTH: 1. Read Chapter 8: "Establishing a Creative Love Life."
2. Fill out Project 8 (checklists).

HUSBAND: Make reservations for overnight. The location should be close by but nice.

WIFE: 1. Make arrangements for children to sleep at a friend's, or arrange for a sitter to come in for the night.
2. Pack a picnic supper to take, and candles too!
3. Take along one book on the sexual relationship in marriage.

ESTABLISHING A CREATIVE LOVE LIFE

All you have to do is to be in the same room with Dick and Nancy to know their relationship is special! They often hold hands, and if you watch closely you can tell that through their glances they pass all kinds of intimate secret messages.

Their sexual relationship is the icing on the cake in their marriage. They share many common interests, but a big one is their love life. They work as hard at their sexual relationship as they do at communicating and resolving conflicts in their marriage. For them it is a real challenge to find new ways of pleasing each other.

From time to time they go away for the weekend just to enjoy one another. It isn't uncommon for Dick to phone Nancy to tell her he loves her and is looking forward to their next lovemaking session. From time to time Dick finds intimate notes in his briefcase from Nancy that let him know he is desired.

Are Dick and Nancy for real? Yes, they are a real couple we know; only the names have been changed. How long would you guess they have been married? One year? Six months? One month? Or do they sound like newlyweds? Would you believe they have been married twenty years!

Perhaps we all have been victimized by comments like the following:

I know you think sex is exciting now, but just wait a couple of years. The novelty will wear off and other things will become more important!

It's O.K. with me if my husband has a mistress as long as he is discreet. It takes the pressure off me.

After you have been married for fifteen years you'll know what I mean—sex is a real bore!

It just didn't work out that great for my wife and me. I think sex in marriage is grossly overrated.

How long to adjust?

We have heard that it takes up to six years for a married couple to adjust sexually, and up to twenty years to fully enjoy each other. How long have you been married? Five years? Do you have five years of expertise in this area or one year's expertise repeated five times? Is your sexual relationship growing or is it always the same? Even eating steak every day for dinner would get boring after a while!

What are you doing to make your marriage a love affair? If you're not to the love affair level with your mate yet, we'd like to help you put romance into your love life. In the following pages we will consider these three areas:

1. God's view of sex (it was His idea in the first place!)
2. How to overcome inhibitions and boredom
3. How to be a creative lover

SEX—GOD'S IDEA

Let's go back to our ultimate marriage manual and look at Genesis 2:24,25: "For this cause a man shall leave his father and his mother, and shall cleave to his wife; and they shall become one flesh. And the man and his wife were both naked and were not ashamed."

Here God put His stamp of approval on the sexual union in marriage. He not only approves of it; He invented it! It is to be an expression of love between husband and wife, fulfilling and enjoyable.

Certainly God intended sex for procreation, but just as certainly He also intended sex for pleasure for *both* husband and wife. Only the man needs to reach orgasm in order for the couple to have children, but God also created woman with the capability of receiving *much* pleasure from the sexual union.

The Bible discusses sex openly and matter-of-factly, acknowledging that it is a precious gift from God. Consider Proverbs 5:18,19: "Let your fountain be blessed, And rejoice in the wife of your youth. As a loving hind and a graceful doe, Let her breasts satisfy you at all times; Be exhilarated always with her love."

Are you exhilarated with your mate's love? Do you satisfy each other? That's God's plan! He intends for your sexual relationship to be enjoyable and exciting.

If you question this, turn to the Song of Solomon and read about the delights of physical unity in marriage. For an eye-opening evening together, read the Song of Solomon out loud to each other from the Living Bible or another modern translation, and do away with any lingering ideas that God doesn't approve of sex or that sex isn't intended to be exciting and exhilarating.

FAREWELL TO BOREDOM AND INHIBITIONS!

Take the SAT

The biggest problems in the area of sex today are due to boredom and inhibitions. To help you determine where you are in this area, take our SAT (Sexual Attitude Test). Give yourself one point for each yes answer and no points for a no answer.

1. Do you enjoy your physical relationship with your mate?
2. Do you think he (or she) enjoys it, too?
3. Do you look forward to the next time of physical intimacy?
4. Has your mate told you that he or she is satisfied with your sexual relationship?
5. Are you satisfied with your sexual relationship?
6. Do you both initiate lovemaking from time to time?
7. Do you plan special times to be alone together?
8. Have you gone off overnight *alone* together in the last six months for the purpose of enjoying each other?
9. Have you indicated to your mate verbally that you desire him or her in the last two weeks?

If you answered yes six or more times, you have a reasonably good attitude toward sex. If your score was lower than six, don't be discouraged. A candid self-appraisal and an effort to modify your attitude toward the sexual relationship in marriage can result in a change in your score in a very short time!

Away with boredom

First, let's consider why so many couples score low on this quiz. Could it be that we are bored with sex? God forbid!

Like Dick and Nancy, Pat and Sue have also been married twenty years. But their story is quite different. In the first months of marriage they tried "doing what comes naturally," but they never met with much success. They would make love, but just as Sue began to get a few feelings it was all over. Hope began to fade and sex became a routine obligation for Sue.

Deep down, Pat knew that sex wasn't very exciting for his wife, but his ego was too fragile to talk about it, lest his fears be confirmed. So they both settled for mediocrity in this area of their marriage. Needless to say, this led to boredom with a capital B. After twenty years, their sex life consisted of ten minutes after the late news, always the same three kisses, four hugs—you get the picture!

What made the difference in these two couples' experiences? Dick and Nancy really worked on their sexual relationship and made it a priority in their relationship, while Pat and Sue just let it happen (or not happen!). Where do we get the idea that we come into marriage with a built-in expertise in this area? We learn in the area of responding sexually in the same way we learn in any other area—by working at it. We certainly wouldn't make the same assumption ("It just happens") in other areas, be it child rearing, our professions, or hanging wallpaper! No, to achieve success in any area requires work, and sex is no exception.

Too often what happens is that other things take precedence over the sexual relationship. Couples vaguely plan to work on this area, but they fail to set aside time to spend alone together.

The message of *Ten Dates for Mates* is that we need to take time for one another. It takes time to communicate, it takes time to work through conflict, and it takes time to build a good sex life. Ten minutes after the late show just won't do. So to keep boredom away, commit yourself to taking the time and effort that is necessary to make sex an exciting part of your marriage. It can happen!

Overcoming inhibitions

Boredom and inhibitions—the two seem to go together. When we overcome our inhibitions we become more willing to try new things and to be creative. The result is that boredom often disappears.

So how do we overcome inhibitions? The Bible gives us the utmost freedom in this area of marriage. It gives no rules, no regulations, and no instructions on positions, foreplay, or frequency of sexual intercourse. The key is that sex is mutually acceptable and desirable to both partners.

How can we overcome inhibitions? We suggest the following five steps:

1. Recognize that you have inhibitions.

2. Determine to change your SAT (Sexual Attitude Test) score.

3. Saturate your mind with God's perspective. Read the Song of Solomon for a start and memorize key verses.

4. Be willing to communicate verbally with your mate about sex.

5. Decide to be God's version of a creative lover!

Sometimes inhibitions flee quickly just by following these steps. In other cases more time is required. Of course, boredom and inhibitions are not the only problems in the sexual relationship, but they are the most common. If you have serious problems in this area, seek out your pastor, doctor, or counselor. Don't settle for the world's boring evaluation of marital sex: it can be so much more!

BECOMING A CREATIVE LOVER

The way to overcome boredom and to rekindle excitement is to begin to be creative in your sex life. This means making this area a priority. It may be wonderful to lick fifteen thousand envelopes for the local service organization, but if all your activities leave you a frazzle at the end of the day you can forget the creative lover bit! Begin by checking your schedule; make sure you have included time alone with your mate to test some of the following creative ideas! After you have carved out the time, decide together to work on this area. Here are some ideas you can start with:

1. Be available to one another. Have you ever been on a diet? What do you think about all the time? Food! When we aren't available to meet our partner's sexual needs, we are putting them on a diet—and guess what they think about all the time. That's right—*sex*!

A friend of ours asked her doctor what he felt was the major sexual problem in marriage. He said half of his patients complained that their mates never bothered them about sex, while the other half complained that their mates bothered them too much about sex. He said that if only he could reshuffle the couples, everyone would be happy!

Perhaps your mate desires sex more or less than you do; here is one place to put to use all those good communication skills you learned on Date 5. It's good to discuss this area openly, but remember that the key is to have the attitude of being available.

2. Be willing to take the initiative!
3. Plan time into your schedule for each other.
   a. Consider a weekend away to enjoy each other.
   b. Plan a couple of hours each week when you can be completely alone.
   c. Don't overlook the possibility of using a friend's empty apartment for a date.
4. Redo your bedroom with lots of candles!
5. Have a lock installed on your bedroom door if there is not one already there. There is nothing quite like privacy.
6. Read books together on this subject.
7. How does your wardrobe look? "Holey" bathrobes and underwear are not exactly sexy!
8. Shape up in the weight department if needed.
9. Kidnap your mate, if he or she likes surprises! One friend of ours made all the arrangements, got a sitter for the children, and surprised his wife with an early anniversary present—three days away to enjoy each other, with no meals to cook, no phones to answer, and no responsibilities.
10. Call your mate to let him or her know you desire him or her.
11. Husband, give your wife an evening off. Clean the kitchen and put the children to bed while she takes a hot oil bath. Add candles to the bathroom decor!
12. Write your mate a love letter.
13. Give your mate an all-over body massage with scented lotion.
14. Spend at least one hour talking and making slow love.
15. Have your mate verbalize what pleases him or her while you make love.
16. Give your mate an unexpected little gift for no reason at all.
17. Buy a new "mood music" tape or record.
18. Tell your mate ten reasons why you love him or her.
19. Make arrangements *now* to go away overnight for Date 8.

It's your choice

Your sexual relationship can be as fulfilling and exciting as you want to make it. But like Dick and Nancy, you will find it takes time and work. But it's worth it; it can become better, more intimate, and more wonderful as the years go on!

PROJECT
ESTABLISHING A CREATIVE LOVE LIFE

Go through the following two checklists, checking yourself in the first list and then checking how you think your wife would rate herself in the second. The following statements are designed to help you evaluate your own attitudes toward the sexual relationship in marriage. They can be a launching pad to new depths of communication in this area with your mate.

A Husband's Checklist

> (O)–Often
> (S)–Sometimes
> (R)–Rarely
> (N)–Never

_____ I enjoy our sexual relationship.

_____ I help my wife to respond sexually.

_____ My priorities and time management interfere with our sexual relationship.

_____ I take the initiative in lovemaking.

_____ I try to be creative in this area.

_____ I know what pleases my wife.

_____ I am a tender lover.

_____ I make it easy for my mate to talk about our sexual relationship.

_____ I let my wife know that I desire her.

_____ I'm willing to work on areas in our sexual relationship that need improvement.

A Wife's Checklist

(O)—Often
(S)—Sometimes
(R)—Rarely
(N)—Never

_____ I enjoy our sexual relationship.

_____ My husband helps me to respond sexually.

_____ Being overtired interferes with our sexual relationship.

_____ I take the initiative in lovemaking.

_____ I try to be creative in this area.

_____ I know what pleases my husband.

_____ I set the atmosphere for our lovemaking—candles, perfume, music, etc.

_____ I make it easy for my husband to talk about our sexual relationship.

_____ I let my husband know that I desire him.

_____ I'm willing to work on areas in our sexual relationship that need improvement.

PROJECT
ESTABLISHING A CREATIVE LOVE LIFE

Go through the following two checklists, checking yourself in the first list and then checking how you think your husband would rate himself in the second. The following statements are designed to help you evaluate your own attitudes toward the sexual relationship in marriage. They can be a launching pad to new depths of communication in this area with your mate.

A Wife's Checklist

> (O)—Often
> (S)—Sometimes
> (R)—Rarely
> (N)—Never

_____ I enjoy our sexual relationship.

_____ My husband helps me to respond sexually.

_____ Being overtired interferes with our sexual relationship.

_____ I take the initiative in lovemaking.

_____ I try to be creative in this area.

_____ I know what pleases my husband.

_____ I set the atmosphere for our lovemaking—candles, perfume, music, etc.

_____ I make it easy for my husband to talk about our sexual relationship.

_____ I let my husband know that I desire him.

_____ I'm willing to work on areas in our sexual relationship that need improvement.

A Husband's Checklist

> (O)–Often
> (S) –Sometimes
> (R)–Rarely
> (N)–Never

_____ I enjoy our sexual relationship.

_____ I help my wife to respond sexually.

_____ My priorities and time management interfere with our sexual relationship.

_____ I take the initiative in lovemaking.

_____ I try to be creative in this area.

_____ I know what pleases my wife.

_____ I am a tender lover.

_____ I make it easy for my mate to talk about our sexual relationship.

_____ I let my wife know that I desire her.

_____ I'm willing to work on areas in our sexual relationship that need improvement.

DATE EIGHT

DATE NIGHT

Go away for a relaxed evening and night together. If this is absolutely impossible, then take a four- to six-hour date to a motel or other very private place. The goal for this date is to have time alone in a relaxed atmosphere away from phone, children, etc.

1. Discuss checklist together. Remember to use the Feelings Formula.

2. Go through Chapter 8 and pick out several ideas that appeal to you, or think up your own. Write out and put in a jar. Draw out potluck and have fun! Away with inhibitions!

3. If you have managed to get away overnight or for a weekend (which we highly recommend), read together a book on sex.

ASSIGNMENT: Read Chapter 9.

EXTRA READING FOR THE EAGER BEAVER

Dillow, Joseph. *Solomon on Sex*. Nashville: Thomas Nelson, 1977.

LaHaye, Tim and Beverly. *The Act of Marriage*. Grand Rapids, Mich.: Zondervan, 1976.

Wheat, Ed and Gaye. *Intended for Pleasure*. Old Tappan, N.J.: Revell, 1977.

DATE NINE

Purposes: 1. To evaluate where we are in our marriage and where we want to be in the future.
2. To set marriage objectives.
3. To set realistic plans for getting there!

Time Commitment: One evening, and one hour of preparation.

Preparation:

BOTH: Read Chapter 9: "An Eye Toward the Future." Read through Project 9 and be ready to fill it out with your mate on Date 9.

AN EYE TOWARD THE FUTURE

Doug and Beth had almost completed their "Ten Dates for Mates." They were both encouraged and enthusiastic about working on their relationship. There were so many good ideas and things they wanted to incorporate into their marriage, but things were getting confusing.

Doug and Beth were each reading several different books on various marital subjects, but they were having difficulty finding time to complete and discuss them with each other. They had planned a "communication date" for this week, but they also needed to plan their vacation and discuss remodeling their bedroom. On Date 8 they had decided to redo their bedroom, and the architect and electrician were coming early in the morning. That meant more deadlines for picking out wallpaper and carpet. They also needed to rework their budget; maybe they could do that next week. If only there were more hours in each day!

Doug had convinced Beth to take tennis lessons, which were to start tomorrow. The exercise would help her on her diet. She had made the commitment to lose ten pounds to please Doug, and he had committed himself to jog three miles each day with their son.

Their attempt to resolve three more areas of conflict had backfired last night—perhaps they both were too tired. Certainly they were trying to improve their marriage. Why wasn't it working?

Mission impossible?

Perhaps things aren't quite as hectic at your house, but do you ever get overcommitted and sidetracked? You start a good project, but you don't seem to make progress because of previous commitments you have made? Instead of controlling your circumstances, the circumstances seem to be controlling you. Like Doug and Beth, you start out to enrich your marriage, but you end up in turmoil and chaos and very, very tired!

What's a couple to do? You wouldn't be this far along in your "Ten Dates" if you weren't serious about improving your marriage. You have a lot of good ideas, but how can you put them all together? How can you avoid chaos and yet deepen your marriage relationship? Let's begin by considering the following three questions:

1. Where are you in your marriage today?
2. Where do you want to be—what style of marriage do you want?
3. How can you devise a plan of action to get where you want to be?

WHERE ARE YOU?

The loudspeaker of the big jet clicked on, and the captain's voice announced: "Now there's no cause for alarm, but we thought you passengers should be informed that for the last two hours we've been flying without the benefit of radio, compass, radar, or navigational beam. This means, in the broadest sense of the word, that we're not sure in which direction we are heading. On the brighter side of the picture, however, I'm sure you'll be interested to know that we are making excellent time!"

In our marriages, it's important not just to be making good time, but to know where we are going. And in order to know how to get where we are going, we need to know where we are right now. To help determine where we are today, let's look again at the Marriage Involvement Chart from Chapter 2.

DEGREES OF INVOLVEMENT IN MARRIAGE

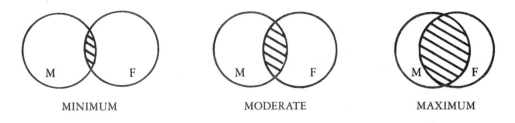

MINIMUM   MODERATE   MAXIMUM

Where are you and your mate in your marriage today? Remember that the key word is *involvement*. Have the past eight dates caused your circles to move closer together?

After going through the previous dates, are you and your mate more in agreement concerning the amount of mutual involvement you both desire for your marriage?

Part 1 of Date 9 will be going back to these circles and determining together what degree of involvement you would like to have and can realistically achieve. This brings us to the second question.

WHERE DO YOU WANT TO BE?

The next step is to discuss with your mate the degree of involvement you both desire. Compromise may be part of the process. Remember the communication techniques you have learned and use them! The next step is to set realistic objectives for your marriage together with your mate. Did we hear you groan? Husband, where would you be in your profession today without planning your objectives and goals? Business thrives on goal-setting, and marriages desperately need more of it! But few are the couples who have ever taken the time to set specific objectives for their marriages, much less drawn up a plan to accomplish them.

What's an objective?

A marriage objective is what you and your mate would like to see happen in your marriage. It is a target toward which you and your mate both agree to work. Let us give you some examples of marriage objectives:

1. To develop a deeper personal relationship with my mate. To develop common interests and get to know my mate better.

2. To improve communication with my mate and to learn to express myself in a better way.

3. To improve and become more creative in our sexual relationship.

4. To become more united and responsible in the area of finances.

5. To commit ourselves more deeply in the area of building one another up and not tearing down.

6. To learn to benefit from my mate's strengths and weaknesses and not be threatened.

7. To learn to resolve conflict in a positive way that builds our relationship instead of tearing it down.

Part 2 of Date 9 will be determining together what objectives you want to set for your marriage. You may write down several objectives, but choose one that you want to work on first. This will help you avoid the problems Doug and Beth were having as they were trying to work on all areas at the same time. So pick your major for the next few months. We suggest starting with an easy area where you can quickly see some progress. As you build your faith level, you can go on to more difficult areas.

HOW ARE YOU GETTING THERE?

Now devise a plan of action to help you reach your objective. Three simple words can guide you through this process:
1. What? 2. How? 3. When?

What?

What is the marriage objective you want to achieve? Write this out under the question "What?" For example, in the area of communication you might write: What? *To improve communication with my mate and to learn to express myself in a better way.*

How?

Logically, the next thing is to ask, "How am I going to reach this objective?" This part needs to be measurable so you'll know when you are there. How are you going to open up communication with your mate? What activities will help you accomplish your goal? For example:

1. For the next ten weeks we will have one date night per week and again work through *Ten Dates for Mates*. (Repetition aids learning!)
2. Plan a weekend away without the children in the next three months.
3. Read two books apiece on communication and discuss with each other. Two suggestions are *To Understand Each Other,* by Paul Tournier, and *Communication: Key to Your Marriage,* by Norman Wright.
4. Practice a communication skill each week. One week you could choose to concentrate on really listening, for example.

When?

Without answering this final question, you probably would not reach your objective. This is the time to pull out your calendars and daily diaries and write in (in ink!) the time for doing the above activities.

Which night of the week is going to be your date night? If it is Tuesday, then write "date night" in your calendar on every Tuesday night. When are you going to manage a weekend away? Pencil in several possibilities and begin working on getting a sitter.

What books on communication are you going to read? Block out time to sit down and read them. List communication skills you would like to work on and assign them a definite week. Now, *commit yourselves to following your plan.*

One final illustration

WHAT? *Marriage Objective:* To improve and become more creative in our sexual relationship.

HOW? *Short-Term Plans:*

1. Read two books on this subject together, such as *Solomon on Sex,* by Joseph Dillow, and *Intended for Pleasure,* by Ed and Gaye Wheat.
2. Set aside two hours each week to have completely alone together for the next ten weeks.
3. Go off for one weekend without the children in the next three months.
4. Try one new creative idea each week.

WHEN? *Scheduling:*

1. Will read together for thirty minutes Monday and Thursday nights before we go to sleep.
2. Husband will arrange his schedule to take two hours for lunch on Fridays. Wife will keep her schedule free for lunch on Fridays!
3. Will plan to go away alone the first weekend next month.
4. Will make a list of creative ideas to try!

What about interruptions?

There is one thing for sure—interruptions *will* appear. There will be some weeks when date night won't happen, due to sick children, drop-in guests, or other unforeseeable events. But even if we don't follow through with every single activity, we will have gone a lot further toward reaching our objective than if we had not planned at all. So be realistic, but also keep on persevering, and you will be the winners!

PROJECT
AN EYE TOWARD THE FUTURE

PART 1

Discuss and determine your style of marriage (degree of involvement).
Where are you?
Where do you want to be?

PART 2

1. Look back through the previous projects and list areas you both agree you would like to work on. Then prioritize them.

A.

B.

C.

D.

E.

From the list above, write out Marriage Objectives.

A.

B.

C.

D.

E.

2. Choose the area you want to work on first. Write out the following (see Chapter 9 for examples):

WHAT?   Long-term marriage objectives
HOW?   Short-term objectives
WHEN?   Fill in on your calendar.

3. Schedule into the next two and a half months the activities listed under short-term objectives.

MONTH: _____

	WEEK	WEEK
Mon.		
Tues.		
Wed.		
Thurs.		
Fri.		
Sat.		
Sun.		

	WEEK	WEEK
Mon.		
Tues.		
Wed.		
Thurs.		
Fri.		
Sat.		
Sun.		

MONTH: _____

	WEEK	WEEK
Mon.		
Tues.		
Wed.		
Thurs.		
Fri.		
Sat.		
Sun.		

	WEEK	WEEK
Mon.		
Tues.		
Wed.		
Thurs.		
Fri.		
Sat.		
Sun.		

MONTH: _____

	WEEK	WEEK
Mon.		
Tues.		
Wed.		
Thurs.		
Fri.		
Sat.		
Sun.		

4. Now make a commitment to yourself, to your wife, and to God that you will follow through with the plans you have made today. As you see improvement in this one area, begin to work on the next one!

PROJECT
AN EYE TOWARD THE FUTURE

PART 1

Discuss and determine your style of marriage (degree of involvement).
Where are you?
Where do you want to be?

PART 2

1. Look back through the previous projects and list areas you both agree you would like to work on. Then prioritize them.

A.

B.

C.

D.

E.

From the list above, write our Marriage Objectives.

A.

B.

C.

D.

E.

2. Choose the area you want to work on first. Write out the following (see Chapter 9 for examples):

WHAT?   Long-term marriage objectives
HOW?   Short-term objectives
WHEN?   Fill in on your calendar.

3. Schedule into the next two and a half months the activities listed under short-term objectives.

MONTH: _____

	WEEK	WEEK
Mon.		
Tues.		
Wed.		
Thurs.		
Fri.		
Sat.		
Sun.		

	WEEK	WEEK
Mon.		
Tues.		
Wed.		
Thurs.		
Fri.		
Sat.		
Sun.		

MONTH: _____

	WEEK	WEEK
Mon.		
Tues.		
Wed.		
Thurs.		
Fri.		
Sat.		
Sun.		

	WEEK	WEEK
Mon.		
Tues.		
Wed.		
Thurs.		
Fri.		
Sat.		
Sun.		

MONTH: _____

	WEEK	WEEK
Mon.		
Tues.		
Wed.		
Thurs.		
Fri.		
Sat.		
Sun.		

4. Now make a commitment to yourself, to your husband, and to God that you will follow through with the plans you have made today. As you see improvement in this one area, begin to work on the next one!

DATE NINE

DATE NIGHT

Go back to your favorite restaurant that you went to on Date 1.

Go through Project 9, setting objectives for your marriage. Choose one and answer the questions, What? How? and When?

ASSIGNMENT: Read Chapter 10.

EXTRA READING FOR THE EAGER BEAVER

Wright, Norman. *The Pillars of Marriage.* Glendale, Calif.: Regal, 1979.

DATE TEN

Purposes: 1. To consider how faith in God relates to marriage.

2. To review things learned in these ten dates.

3. To recommit myself to my mate and marriage and to our plan of action for continuing.

Time Commitment: One evening, and one hour of preparation.

Preparation:

BOTH: Read Chapter 10: "Toward Christian Marriage." Fill out Project 10.

TOWARD CHRISTIAN MARRIAGE

For ten dates we have been concentrating on teaming up. We hope you now have a strategy for winning, including much better communication. Even when you disagree, you can work it out without hurting your relationship. You've learned to benefit from each other's strengths and weaknesses and you've got your roles down. Your game has definitely improved and the future looks bright. How can you be sure that the progress you've made is lasting—that once the pages of *Ten Dates for Mates* are closed the principles learned will not be forgotten?

The one element in our own marriage that has given us the power to keep on applying the principles we have learned is our relationship with Jesus Christ. Without Him, *Ten Dates* can be just another attempt at finding a meaningful relationship along with open marriage, women's liberation, and sex techniques.

In our hearts we believe it is time to get back to the basics, back to the One who created marriage in the first place. God has given us the principles in His marriage book, the Bible. But beyond that, He wants to give us the power to carry out His principles through being personally involved in our marriages and in our lives. He wants to have a personal relationship with each of us through His Son, Jesus Christ. And not only does He want to give us the power to implement His principles in our marriages, but He also wants to give us purpose and meaning in our lives.

What's real security?

On Date 4 we talked about building a sense of self-worth in ourselves and in our mates. Another way of achieving self-worth is through security and significance. We each need to have a sense of security along with a good self-image, and we encouraged you to build one another up in this area. We can help build self-worth in our mates, but ultimately we must look to God for total fulfillment in this area. No matter how great our mates are, there are some needs that they simply can't meet in our lives—only God can.

Our need for security demands that we be loved unconditionally. Have you ever tried to love your mate unconditionally? You get an extra point for trying, but only God can offer us that kind of love! His love was so unconditional that He was willing to give His only Son for a world that had rejected Him.

Consider John 3:16: "For God so loved the world, that He gave His only begotten Son, that whoever believes in Him should not perish, but have eternal life." You probably memorized that verse in Sunday school as a child; but stop for a minute and in place of the words *the world,* put your name. Nothing we will ever do will cause God to stop loving us. Consider also Romans 8:38,39:

> For I am convinced that neither death, nor life, nor angels, nor principalities, nor things present, nor things to come, nor powers, nor height, nor depth, nor any other created thing, shall be able to separate us from the love of God, which is in Christ Jesus our Lord.

Talk about real security—that's it! Even John Lennon, in one of his most popular Beatles songs, wrote, "All we need is love!" If people in the world today are so aware of this need for love, why aren't we experiencing God's unconditional love in our lives? Let us suggest two possible reasons:

1. Perhaps we've never fully understood why Christ came and what the issue really is. Consider these facts:

    A. Jesus is fully God and fully man.

    B. He lived a perfect life.

    C. He died in our place.

    D. He rose from the dead and is alive today.

2. Perhaps you have chosen to go your own way, like the defiant teenager who said, "No thanks, God, I'd rather do it myself!"

If you're in the second category, it is time to reevaluate any lingering adolescent rebellion and consider the facts once again. Maybe you've rejected a caricature of what you think Christianity is without really considering Christ.

More likely, you are in the first category like we were, and you just need more information. Let us share with you a recent experience in our home that will help illustrate what we are talking about.

Broken Horses

One of our favorite souvenirs of our years in Europe is a ceramic horse that lives on our sofa table. He was purchased at the ceramic factory as a factory second. He had a patched-up broken leg, but we didn't care. He was still very special to us.

Our horse had several close calls, living with three active boys and all their friends. Well, a few weeks ago it finally happened: Mr. Horse took a fall, and all the king's horses and all the Arp men couldn't put our horse together again. You might say our horse "went to pieces," and there were many of them! We gathered up all the pieces and began to try to put the puzzle together, but it looked like an impossible job.

At this point we had several alternatives:

1. We could say, "Accidents happen. It's broken too badly to ever repair. Let's throw it away," and toss it into the trash.

2. We could bring out the Super Glue and try to glue all the pieces back together again. This might have worked for a while, but the next time a little stress was put on the horse he probably would have broken again. Have you ever tried to reglue something you've already glued once?

3. We could take our broken horse to a person who makes ceramic horses and let him put it together again. He is the one who creates ceramic horses in the first place, and he understands all about horses and how they are to go together.

A family conference was called and it was unanimously decided to take the horse to the expert and have it repaired. This we did, and we just got our horse back last week. You should see it—it's even prettier than before! It no longer has a broken leg. The horse specialist remolded the broken parts and refired the horse so that it is impossible to see where the leg was broken. If we didn't know better, we would have thought he just gave us a new horse! We were all thrilled—except for the bill that accompanied our restored horse. Believe us, it was costly! We all went to work saving money, and after a few less visits to McDonald's and some other family contributions, we now own a very special expensive horse.

Repaired lives

Not only is our horse special because it is a memory of our time in Europe, but it is also a picture of what God has done for us and is willing to do for anyone who asks.

Look around you today and you will see broken lives—just as broken as our horse was.

In Romans 3:23 we read: "For all have sinned and fall short of the glory of God." Perhaps you are like we were, and the word *sin* doesn't really relate very well to you. Let us list some symptoms of sin that helped us to better understand this verse— worry, irritability, lack of purpose in life, envy, jealousy, self-centeredness, impure thoughts, critical spirit, discouragement. Basically, sin is going our own way, completely indifferent to God. Our rebellion may be active and noticeable to other people, or it can be a passive indifference on the inside. Whatever form it takes, sin leads to broken lives.

As with our horse, there are basically three options open to us:

1. We can say, "My life is all broken and messed up. There's really nothing that can be done. I won't even try!" Many people today are throwing away their lives because they simply don't realize there are other options!

2. The second approach many people try is a do-it-yourself repair program. Self-reform may look like it is working for a while, but when the stresses and strains of life come along we find our lives are more broken than before, with little hope for change.

3. The third option is to take the broken pieces of our lives to the Master and let Him put them together again! God is the specialist—He made us in the first place and He has the master plan of what our lives are supposed to be. He specialized in putting broken lives and marriages back together. He knows how to remold the broken parts, how to refire them, how to make them strong and able to withstand the stresses and strains of life.

It is costly

God has the power to put us together again and give us new lives, and like our horse, this new birth is very costly. But unlike our horse, we can never pay for it! The good news is that God has already paid dearly by sacrificing His only Son, Jesus Christ, in our place. When Jesus died on the cross, He paid in full all the expenses involved in giving us new lives—the beginning of a new life here and eternal life forever with God. Romans 5:8 tells us: "But God demonstrates His own love toward us, in that while we were yet sinners, Christ died for us."

If God has paid in advance, what is our part?

Our Part

Our part is to individually receive Jesus Christ into our lives and allow Him to begin putting them back together. Receiving Christ is not an emotional experience or a feeling. You do not have to don black robes and pray all day. Neither is it being hit by a bolt of lightning. Receiving Christ is a volitional commitment that involves a response on our part.

In Revelation 3:20 we read: "Behold, I stand at the door and knock; if anyone hears My voice and opens the door, I will come in to him." Christ stands at the door of each life, but the handle is on the inside. What responses are open to you?

1. You could say, "No, go away!"
2. You could ignore the knock, which is basically the same as saying no.
3. You could open the door and invite Him in.

Christ is knocking at the door of your heart. What is your response? To ignore Him is to reject Him! We receive Christ through faith, which can be expressed by prayer. Prayer is simply talking to God. He is not so concerned with your words as He is with the attitude of your heart. Here is a suggested prayer:

Lord Jesus, I need You. I open the door of my heart and receive You as my Savior and Lord. Thank You for dying for me and for forgiving my sins. Take control of my life and make me and my marriage into what You desire it to be. Thank You for coming into my life like You promised in Your Word You would do if I asked in faith.

If this expresses how you feel, then pray this prayer right now and Christ will come into your life as he promised.

Now what?

When we invite Christ into our lives we may see a sudden change, but more likely it will be a gradual change. Remember, Christianity is not a feeling; it is a commitment to let God run our lives and put them back together. How does all of this relate to marriage? Consider the following illustration:

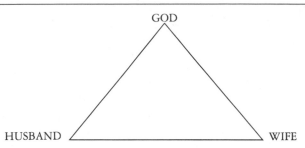

A winning marriage team involves three players. The husband is on one side and the wife is on the other, and God is at the top. As the husband and wife grow closer to God, they will also grow closer together. With God as your marriage coach, you are on the way to a winning streak!

Let's review

The past ten dates have given you the advantage of better understanding your mate. You are able to express your feelings and even to disagree in a constructive way. You know your appropriate role. You are familiar with God's marriage principles and know how He can fit into your life and marriage through a personal relationship with Jesus Christ. You have a plan for the future and have passed your SATs. But before we give you your diploma, we have one final test for you. To score, give yourself ten points for each yes answer.

_____ 1. I have enjoyed the last nine dates with my mate. It is a habit I want to continue.

_____ 2. I have learned some new insights about my mate that I didn't know or understand previously.

_____ 3. We have resolved together one conflict in our marriage during the past nine dates.

_____ 4. I have used the Feelings Formula successfully (no knock-down, drag-out fights!).

_____ 5. I am more aware of our individual strengths and weaknesses.

_____ 6. We have tried at least one new creative intimate play and have raised my SAT score (if it was low).

_____ 7. We have set objectives for our marriage and have concrete plans to work on one area in the next weeks and months.

_____ 8. We have discussed and agree on our style of marriage (degree of involvement).

_____ 9. I am willing in the future to give up something I want to do in order to do something my mate wants to do.

_____ 10. We're winning more games than we're losing, and I am committed to my mate.

Add up your score and let's see how you did! Rate your score on the following scale:

100	Fantastic! You qualify as a *Ten Dates for Mates* guide. Run out and find another couple to personally escort through *Ten Dates for Mates*!
80–90	Great! You're well on your way to winning the marriage game. Keep up the good work and stick to your plan!
60–70	Not bad. Don't give up. Pick out the weak areas and continue to work!
50 or below	Turn back to page one.

Whatever your score, by completing these ten dates you have shown you have what it takes to become a winning team. Congratulations! You are now a *Ten Dates for Mates* alumnus. With the title comes the responsibility to continue in the things you have learned and to pass them on to other couples. Count your marriage among the winners!

PROJECT
TOWARD CHRISTIAN MARRIAGE

1. What was your favorite date and why?

2. What new insights have you gained . . .
   A. . . . about your wife?

   B. . . . about yourself?

3. What is your perspective of the role of Jesus Christ in your marriage? In your own life?

4. Are you willing to commit yourself in a new way to your wife by actively adhering to the principles learned and practiced in the past nine dates?

5. What night have you chosen for your date night next week?

PROJECT
TOWARD CHRISTIAN MARRIAGE

1. What was your favorite date and why?

2. What new insights have you gained . . .
   A. . . . about your husband?

   B. . . . about yourself?

3. What is your perspective of the role of Jesus Christ in your marriage? In your own life?

4. Are you willing to commit yourself in a new way to your husband by actively adhering to the principles learned and practiced in the past nine dates?

5. What night have you chosen for your date night next week?

DATE TEN

DATE NIGHT

You're on your own! Choose your favorite place.
Work through and discuss Project 10.

ASSIGNMENT

Continue to put into practice all the things you have learned. Follow your plan of action from Date 9.

EXTRA READING FOR THE EAGER BEAVER

Bright, Bill. *Transferable Concepts Series.* San Bernardino, Calif.: Campus Crusade, 1981.

Lewis, C.S. *Mere Christianity.* New York: Macmillan, 1964.